Survival Tips for

PUBLIC

SPEAKING

Wendy H. Papa
Ohio University

KENDALL/HUNT PUBLISHING COMPANY
4050 Westmark Drive   Dubuque, Iowa 52002

CONTENTS

Organizing Materials: Arranging the Trip

Audio and Visual Elements: Sights and Sounds   65

Language: The Vehicle for Your Trip

Delivery: Plans into Action   79

Informative Speaking: Special Precautions   89

Persuasive Speaking: Navigating the Territory   95

PREFACE

This book was developed to enhance the understanding and application of the content of Public Speaking.

The book is designed to help students:

1. Understand course requirements and philosophy.

2. Understand the criteria for the evaluation of each oral and written assignment.

3. Promote thinking and application of concepts through chapter review questions and individual activities.

4. Utilize experiential activities to further clarify concepts.

5. Provide suggested outline formats.

6. Utilize specific knowledge objectives and concepts for the purpose of study and review.

TO MAXIMIZE THE VALUE OF THESE MATERIALS,
THIS BOOK SHOULD BE BROUGHT TO CLASS EACH DAY.

Wendy H. Papa, Ph.D.
Course Director
School of Interpersonal Communication
Ohio University
Athens, Ohio

Speech Assignments

Note: Instructors reserve the right to choose among the following alternatives.

Demonstration

Definition: The Demonstration speech is an informative speech in which you show the audience an object, a person, or a place; in which you show the audience how something works; in which you show the audience how to do something; or in which you show the audience why something occurs. The focus in the speech of demonstration is on the visualization of your topic. Students will be required to bring any appropriate presentational aides to class. The University prohibits firearms, drugs and other illegal contraband in the classroom.

Time Requirement: 5-7 minutes

Outline: full content, sentence format

Bibliography: sources are to be listed according to APA

Source Requirement: Minimum of 3 sources (library or interview)

Point Value: speech = 80 points and outline = 20 points

Informative

Definition: The purpose of the informative speech is to convey information and to do so clearly, accurately, and interestingly. The goal is not to alter the listeners' attitudes or behaviors but to facilitate their understanding of the subject and their ability to retain this new information. Although several classifications of informative speeches are possible, our text examines four types: *demonstration*, *explanation*, *self-description*, and *presentation of statistical information*.

Time Requirement: 5-7 minutes

Outline: full content, sentence format

Bibliography: sources are to be listed according to APA

Source Requirement: minimum of 5 sources (library or interview)

Point Value: speech = 80 points and outline = 20 points

Persuasive

Definition: A speech to persuade seeks to influence either beliefs or actions. The three purposes of persuasive speaking are to *shape* audience responses toward some predetermined goal; *reinforce* audience responses by rewarding the audience for sustaining their present beliefs, attitudes, and values; and *change* audience responses, altering an audience's behavior toward a product, concept, or idea.

Time Requirement: 5-7 minutes

Outline: full content, sentence format

Bibliography: sources are to be listed according to APA

Source Requirement: minimum of 5 sources (library or interview)

Point Value: speech = 80 points and outline = 20 points

Speeches of Refutation

Definition: The purpose of the speeches of refutation is to work with another student to select a disputable topic and to phrase a specific purpose that confirms or changes a belief, such as "Employers should be prohibited from administering random drug tests to their employees" or "The Catholic church should ordain women into the priesthood." You may want to discuss the wording with your instructor. Make sure you phrase the specific purpose so that the first speaker is in favor of the proposal. The first speaker will then give a five to seven minute persuasive speech offering at least three arguments for the proposal. The second speaker will give a five to seven minute speech opposing the specific arguments presented by the first speaker.

Time Requirement: 5-7 minutes

Outline: full content, sentence format

Bibliography: sources are to listed according to APA

Source Requirement: minimum of 5 sources (library or interview)

Point Value: speech = 80 points and outline = 20 points

Problem and Solution Speeches

Definition: The purpose of the problem and solution speeches is to convince your audience of a need to act (problem speech) and a means to act (solution speech).

The Problem Speech (first speech) illustrates a problem affecting your audience and why this problem won't go away without attention from your audience. This speech should contain at least two main points. One main point must explain the scope and nature of the problem. A second main point must explain why the problem will not go away without our action.

Time Requirement: 5-7 minutes

Outline: full content, sentence format

Bibliography: sources are to be listed according to APA

Source Requirement: minimum of 5 sources (library or interview)

Point Value: speech = 80 points and outline = 20 points

The Solution Speech (second speech) is a speech in which you revise your problem speech (addressing its weaknesses) and add a solution which your audience can enact to help solve the problem. Therefore, this speech contains the two main points addressed in your problem speech with a third point that explains how the problem can be solved. Individual initiatives should be identified in this point. *The most effective solution speeches will follow the format of Monroe's motivated sequence.

Time Requirement: 5-7 minutes

Outline: full content, sentence format

Bibliography: sources are to be listed according to APA

Source Requirement: minimum of 5 sources (library or interview)

Point Value: speech = 80 points and outline = 20 points

Monroe's Motivated Sequence Speech

Definition: Monroe's Motivated Sequence is developed according to five steps that build upon one another: (1) getting the audience's attention, (2) establishing a need, (3) offering a proposal to satisfy the need, (4) inviting listeners to visualize the results, and (5) requesting action.

Time Requirement: 5-7 minutes

Outline: full content, sentence format

Bibliography: sources are to be listed according to APA

Source Requirement: minimum of 5 sources (library or interview)

Point Value: speech = 80 points and outline = 20 points

Special Occasion Speech

Definition: Speeches for special occasions are similar to other types of speeches in that all public presentations call for some information and some persuasion. However, speeches for special occasions are distinguished by the unique situations in which they are presented and by how speakers address each distinctive situation. Special occasions for speech making occur frequently. For example, you may be asked to give a toast to the bride and groom at a close friend's wedding, a eulogy at a deceased relative's funeral, a brief speech introducing the main speaker at a meeting, an acceptance speech to thank an association for an award, an inspirational speech to lift the morale of fellow employees or an entertaining speech at a community service banquet. Although several classifications of special occasion speeches are possible, the most common choices include: the *speech of introduction, welcome, inspiration, farewell, presentation, acceptance, tribute, entertainment*, and the *eulogy.*

Time Requirement: 5-7 minutes

Outline: full content, sentence format

Bibliography: sources are to listed according to APA

Source Requirement: minimum of 5 sources (library or interview)

Point Value: speech = 80 points and outline = 20 points

Improving a Prior Speech

Definition: Now that speeches have been presented, the next speech alternative allows the student to improve a prior speech. Each student will choose one of the prior speeches presented (Demonstration, Informative, Persuasive Speech, or Special Occasion) and refine that speech. First, the student will reflect on the strengths, weaknesses, and recommendations made by the instructor and class peers. Next, the student will rewrite and represent the speech taking into consideration the necessary improvements. This renovation goes beyond adding a few sources, changing some words and correcting an occasional sentence. Effective speakers revise their work, reorganize their material, hone their arguments, vary their support material, and rewrite whole sections to clarify meaning for their listeners. The goal of this speech is to show improvement. Even a great speech can be made better!

Time Requirement: 5-7 minutes

Outline: full content, sentence format

Bibliography: sources are to be listed according to APA

Source Requirement: minimum of 5 sources (library or interview)

Point Value: speech = 80 points and outline = 20 points

Student Information Sheet

(Please Print)

Name: _____

Campus or local address: _____

Local Phone Number: _____

E-Mail Address: _____

Circle One: Male   Female

Circle One: Freshman   Sophomore   Junior   Senior

My major (or my major interest) is _____

_____

I am enrolled in Ohio University because _____

_____

_____

When I think about speaking in public...

I am _____

_____

I am not _____

_____

I can _____

_____

I cannot _____

_____

I want _____

_____

Starting Out

The Process of Communication:
The Basics for the Trip

Chapter 1 Review Questions

Name _____

Upon completion of reading these two chapters, answer the questions below. Be prepared to discuss your responses in class. Use your answers as a study guide for the final examination.

1. Identify the three differences between public speaking and interpersonal communication.

2. What are the reasons for studying public speaking? What are the short term benefits? What are the long term benefits?

3. Identify some of the common misconceptions about public speaking?

Chapter 2 Review Questions

4. Define *communication* according to our text. What are the three key elements of the definition. Provide an example for each.

5. Identify the four elements of our *inner environment* that are particularly useful for our study of communication. Provide an example for each.

6. Explain the differences among *relaying*, *externalizing*, *stimulating*, and *activating*. What do these four functions of communication have in common?

Communicative Functions Activity

Name_____

1. Communication acts can be classified according to four functions: *relaying, externalizing, stimulating,* and *activating.* Identify four different interpersonal interactions you have had in the recent past that exemplify each of these four functions. What was the purpose for each interaction.

    Relaying

    Externalizing

    Stimulating

    Activating

2. Describe four different learning experiences you recently encountered that represent each of the four communication functions. The learning experiences may have been in a classroom, on the playing field, in a church, or at an organized social activity. What was the purpose for each interaction?

Relaying

Externalizing

Stimulating

Activating

Public Speaking in My Life Activity

Name _____

Interview a professor who is an educator within your major. Ask him or her the following questions:

1. How will I use public speaking in my professional life?

2. How often do you think I will need to give some form of a public speech?

3. What kind of speeches will I most likely present?

4. What challenges will I encounter when preparing and presenting a speech?

5. Do you have any advice to offer students of public speaking?

Interview an individual who is a practicing professional in the field of your choice. Ask him or her the following questions:

1. How do you use public speaking in your professional life? In your personal life?

2. How often do you have to give some form of a public speech?

3. What kind of speeches do you give?

4. What challenges do you encounter when preparing and presenting a speech?

5. Do you have any advice to offer students of public speaking?

Who Is in the Class?
An Ice Breaker

Objective: To facilitate the "getting-to-know-you" process in a classroom experience.

Procedure: Take out the *Who is in the class?* work sheet (next page) while your instructor reads the following directions:

"Choose any ten of the items by placing an *X* in front of each of your selections. During the autograph searching session, you will be interviewing other students to find one person who fits each of the following ten categories you have selected. You will then obtain that person's autograph in the appropriate space. Get one signature per item, try not to use duplicate signatures."

When almost all of the students have completed the task, your instructor will call for everyone's attention and end the activity. Any member who has an autograph missing can ask the entire group to find an appropriate person to sign.

Your instructor will lead the class in debriefing this activity.

Discussion Questions:

1. How did you feel about completing the work sheet?
2. What level of risk did you take with signing your name? How do you think that compares with the risks you take in making new acquaintances?
3. How do you feel about the number of signatures you got? What answers surprised you most about your fellow classmates?

Materials Required: *Who is in the Class?* handout (see next page)

Time Required: Approximately 20 minutes

Source: Adapted from Pfeiffer, J.W. & Jones, J.E. (1980). *The 1980 annual handbook for group facilitators*. San Diego, CA: University Associates, Inc.

"Who Is in the Class?"

1. Who has more than 3 siblings _____

2. Who enjoys spicy food _____

3. Who is from a state other than Ohio _____

4. Who is from Athens, Ohio _____

5. Who thinks the President is doing a good job _____

6. Who works on weekends _____

7. Who lives alone _____

8. Who plays a musical instrument _____

9. Who watches *Letterman* or *Leno* regularly _____

10. Who views *Today* or *Good Morning America* regularly _____

11. Who sleeps on a futon _____

12. Who has traveled outside the U.S. _____

13. Who plays on an O.U. athletic team _____

14. Who is a vegetarian _____

15. Who speaks another language _____

16. Who is born under my astrological sign _____

17. Who adores animals _____

18. Who likes to read novels _____

19. Who enjoys going to the movies _____

20. Who loves Public Speaking _____

Making Ethical Choices:
Finding the "Right" Way Dealing with Anxiety

Chapter 3 Review Questions   Name _____

Upon completion of reading these two chapters, answer the questions below. Be prepared to discuss your responses in class. Use your answers as a study guide for the final examination.

1. Why should we study ethics? Why do we need guidelines or standards in ethics? Who sets the ethical standards in the field of communication?

2. Identify the importance of choice for both speakers and listeners. What is the difference between rapist, seducer, and lover communicators.

3. Why do public speakers need to avoid plagiarism and cheating? Provide examples of plagiarism and cheating in a public speaking class. What can happen to a student who is caught plagiarizing or cheating?

Appendix Review Questions

4. What is communication apprehension? Discern the difference between state apprehension and trait apprehension. Do you experience speech apprehension? What type of apprehension do you experience?

5. Identify the typical ways in which speakers can control apprehension. What strategies will you take to control your speaking apprehension? What strategies should you avoid?

6. Is apprehension inevitable? Can apprehension be necessary for good communication? How? Why?

What Are Your Key Values?

Instructions

Below is a list of personal values common to all of us. Consider which values you find most important to you, and rank the top five, generally speaking, with 1 being the most important. Although many of the values listed below will be important to you, choose only the five you feel are *most* important in how you live your life.

—— Family

—— Patriotism

—— Wealth

—— Status

—— Health

—— Cleanliness

—— Individuality

—— Attractiveness

—— Generosity

—— Loyalty

—— Religion (spirituality)

—— Love

—— Knowledge (education)

—— Friendship

—— Being ethical (truthfulness, trustworthiness)

—— Forgiveness

—— Humility

—— Patience

—— Tradition

—— Obeying the Law

—— Hard work

—— Getting along with others

—— Saving face

Interpretation

Once you've completed this very difficult task (hard to select only five, right?), compare your answers with those of your classmates. How do your own priorities overlap or differ with others' based on gender, race, religious background, ethnicity, and age? Why do you think this is so?

How frequently does the value being ethical appear on others' lists? How prominent a value is being ethical to you? How important is this value to you when it comes to your perceptions of the following people:

- President of the United States

- Your best friend

- Your boss

- Your spouse or significant other

- Your advisor

- Colleagues in your profession

- Your parents

- Your instructor in this class

Notice how this list of values is common across all people. That is, each characteristic on the list is something we all value, yet each of us ranks the values on the list somewhat differently. How might our different rankings influence how we communicate with or perceive one another?

Kearney, P., & Plax, T.G. (1996). *Public speaking in a diverse society*. Mountain View, CA: Mayfield Publishing Company.

Personal Report of Communication Apprehension

Please indicate the degree to which each of the following statements apply to you by writing the number showing whether you:

1-strongly agree   2-agree   3-undecided   4-disagree   5-strongly disagree

_____ 1. I dislike participating in group discussions.

_____ 2. Generally, I am comfortable while participating in group discussions.

_____ 3. I am tense and nervous while participating in group discussions.

_____ 4. I like to get involved in group discussions.

_____ 5. Engaging in group discussion with new people makes me tense and nervous.

_____ 6. I am calm and relaxed while participating in group discussions.

_____ 7. Generally, I am nervous when I have to participate in a meeting.

_____ 8. Usually I am calm and relaxed while participating in meetings.

_____ 9. I am calm and relaxed when called upon to express opinions in meetings.

_____ 10. I am afraid to express myself at meetings.

_____ 11. Communicating at meetings usually makes me uncomfortable.

_____ 12. I am very relaxed when answering questions at a meeting.

_____ 13. While in a conversation with a new acquaintance, I feel very nervous.

_____ 14. I have no fear of speaking up in conversations.

_____ 15. Ordinarily I am very tense and nervous in conversations.

_____ 16. Ordinarily I am very calm and relaxed in conversations.

_____ 17. While conversing with a new acquaintance, I feel very relaxed.

_____ 18. I'm afraid to speak up in conversations.

_____ 19. I have no fear of giving a speech.

_____ 20. Certain parts of my body feel very tense and rigid while giving a speech.

_____ 21. I feel relaxed while giving a speech.

_____ 22.   My thoughts become confused and jumbled when I am giving a speech.

_____ 23.   I face the prospect of giving a speech with confidence.

_____ 24.   While giving a speech, I get so nervous I forget facts I really know.

To calculate your score for each of the four communication contexts measured by this instrument, add or subtract your scores for each item as described below. Begin your adding or subtracting with 18 points in each case.

Group Discussion	18 points + scores for items 2, 4, 6 - scores for items 1, 3, 5 Your Group Score = _____
Meetings	18 points + scores for items 8, 9, 12 - scores for items 7, 10, 11 Your Meeting Score = _____
Interpersonal Communication	18 points + scores for items 14, 16, 17 - scores for items 13, 15, 18 Your Dyadic score = _____
Public Speaking	18 points + scores for items 19, 21, 23 - scores for items 20, 22, 24 Your Public Speaking score = _____

Overall Communication Apprehension (CA) = the sum of your subscores: Group + Meeting + Dyadic + Public. Your total CA score = _____ .

Norms for the PRCA-24

Range of Scores:	24-120
Average Score:	65 (plus or minus 15)
High Level of Communication Apprehensive	above 80
Low Level of Communication Apprehensive	below 50

McCroskey, J.C. (1982). *Introduction to rhetorical communication* (4th ed.). Englewood Cliffs, NJ: Prentice-Hall.

A Physiological Approach to Nervousness

Listed below are eight commonly experienced symptoms of speech anxiety. Although the aids provided may not remove the anxiety completely, they could provide enough relief to help you relax and delivery an effective speech.

Fast Beating Heart

cause: The breathing rate speeds up and the heart must supply more blood to the lungs to absorb the increase in oxygen.

cure: a.   slow down the breathing rate
            b.   take deeper breaths
            c.   relax your muscles

Sweating Palms

cause: The increase in temperature of moisture passing over the sweat glands (0.3 degrees to 0.8 degrees F); the hands show this reaction first because they have more concentrated number of sweat glands (370 per square inch).

cure: a.   relax all the muscles that you can
            b.   breathe slowly and decrease the rate of the heart
            c.   move the hands and the fingers

Loss of Breath

cause: When the breathing rate speeds up, unconsciously it becomes very shallow; when you begin to talk you have less than the normal amount of air in your lungs making it difficult to finish longer sentences.

cure: a.   concentrate on breathing slowly and deeply
            b.   pause appropriately during sentences

Cold Sweat

cause: The nerves stimulate the sweat glands which in turn produce excessive perspiration. Since sweat is produced to cool the body, and the body does not need to be cooled, it will feel "clammy" and moist.

cure: a.   convince yourself mentally that the situation will not be traumatic
            b.   relax physically
            c.   engage the hands, if possible, in some type of movement
            d.   move the legs and torso slightly

Weak Knees

cause: The tenseness in the muscles (due to the nervous condition) is allowed to build up (due to lack of movement). When pressure (movement) is applied, instability of the muscles results.

cure: a.   relax physically
            b.   move slowly when you rise to speak
            c.   slightly bend the legs when speaking, don't lock your knees.

Shaky Voice

cause: When you inhale and exhale too much air, your voice muscles become tense. This excessive tension in the larynx, tightens the vocal cords.

cure: a.   stop your speech for 5-10 seconds until you regain control
          b.   breath slowly from your diaphragm
          c.   relax the throat by stifling a yawn as you are moving to the lectern
          d.   realize that your voice does not sound as bad as you think it does

Tight Throat

cause: The muscles in the throat, as in the body, are tensed because of the brain stimuli (this is also the cause of the *lump in the throat*).

cure: a.   relax the shoulders
          b.   stifle a yawn as you move to the lectern
          c.   move your head back and forth and up and down

Dry Mouth and Throat

cause: The secondary function of parts of the throat are to lubricate it; when nervousness occurs, this function is alleviated by others more important (i.e. energy, blood).

cure: a.   move the jaw back and forth
          b.   attempt to swallow three times
          c.   keep the mouth shut before you are to speak
          d.   chew gum (remove it before you speak)
          e.   press the top of your tongue to the roof of your mouth, or lightly bite the inside of your cheek until you salivate

Adapted from Roberts, E.A. (1980-1981) *Instructor's handbook for public speaking InCo 103.* Unpublished manuscript, Ohio University, College of Communication, Athens, OH.

Learning to Listen:
An Essential for the Trip

Criticism: Evaluating the Trip

Chapter 4 Review Questions

Name _____

Upon completion of reading these two chapters, answer the questions below. Be prepared to discuss your responses in class. Use your answers as a study guide for the final examination.

1. How does listening work? Differentiate the three processes that are involved when we are listening.

2. Read the example of *Speaker's Words: Listener's Thoughts* on page 46. Identify your greatest personal difficulty in listening to others. Provide an example of your most embarrassing "poor listening" experience. Explain what went wrong.

3. Identify several ways in which listening can be improved. What role do nonverbal signals play in the listening process? Explain how effective communication is a shared responsibility between listener and speaker.

Chapter 15 Review Questions

4. Identify at least three practical benefits from criticism and evaluation of others' speeches. When have you critically analyzed a speaker? What did you learn from your evaluation?

5. Review the various critical perspectives used by critics to assess speeches. Among these viewpoints, which perspectives are particularly noteworthy to you?

6. What is the functional approach to criticism? Identify and define the specific features that would be important to the critic of any speech. Which feature is most important to you? Why?

Listening Self-Evaluation

How often do you indulge in the following ten bad listening habits? Check yourself carefully on each one:

Habit	Frequency					Score
	Almost Always	Usually	Sometimes	Seldom	Almost Never	
1. Giving in to mental distractions	_____	_____	_____	_____	_____	_____
2. Giving in to physical distractions	_____	_____	_____	_____	_____	_____
3. Trying to recall everything a speaker says	_____	_____	_____	_____	_____	_____
4. Rejecting a topic as uninteresting before hearing the speaker	_____	_____	_____	_____	_____	_____
5. Faking paying attention	_____	_____	_____	_____	_____	_____
6. Jumping to conclusions about a speaker's meaning	_____	_____	_____	_____	_____	_____
7. Deciding a speaker is wrong before hearing everything she or he has to say	_____	_____	_____	_____	_____	_____
8. Judging a speaker on personal appearance	_____	_____	_____	_____	_____	_____
9. Not paying attention to a speaker's evidence	_____	_____	_____	_____	_____	_____
10. Focusing on deliver rather than on what the speaker says	_____	_____	_____	_____	_____	_____
					Total	

How to score:

For every "almost always" checked, give yourself a score of   2

For every "usually" checked, give yourself a score of   4

For every "sometimes" checked, give yourself a score of   6

For every "seldom" checked, give yourself a score of   8

For every "almost never" checked, give yourself a score of   10

Interpretation:

Below 70   You need lots of training in listening.

From 71-90   You listen well.

Above 90   You listen exceptionally well.

Source: Lucas, S.E. (1995). *The art of public speaking: Instructor's manual* (5th. ed.). New York: McGraw Hill.

Adapted from Steil, L.K., Barker, L.L. and Watson, K.W. (1983). *Effective listening*. New York: Random House.

Speech Critique

Your instructor may ask you to critique speeches. Using this speech critique form, evaluate the speakers' presentations.

　　　　　　　+ excellent　　　　　✓ competent　　　　　- needs improvement

Topic _____ Specific Purpose _____

_____ Introduction gained attention

_____ Introduction revealed the topic clearly

_____ Introduction related the topic to the audience

_____ Introduction established credibility for the speaker

_____ Introduction previewed the body of the speech

List the main points of the speech. On the line at the right, note the kinds of supporting materials used for each main point:

　　　　　　　S-statistics　　　　　E-examples　　　　　T-testimony

I. _____ _____

II. _____ _____

III. _____ _____

IV. _____ _____

_____ Speaker maintained strong eye contact

_____ Speaker had sufficient vocal variety (not monotone)

_____ Speaker articulated words clearly (not too soft/fast)

_____ Speaker was conversational (did not read speech)

_____ Speaker seemed poised and confident

_____ Speaker used appropriate gestures/physical movement

_____ Speaker used proper language and grammar

_____ Conclusion reinforced the central idea

_____ Conclusion ended on a strong note

Overall evaluation　　A　A-　B+　B　B-　C+　C　C-　D+　D　D-　F

Speech Critique

+ excellent   ✓ competent   - needs improvement

Topic _____ Specific Purpose _____

_____ Introduction gained attention

_____ Introduction revealed the topic clearly

_____ Introduction related the topic to the audience

_____ Introduction established credibility for the speaker

_____ Introduction previewed the body of the speech

List the main points of the speech. On the line at the right, note the kinds of supporting materials used for each main point:

         S-statistics   *E-examples*   *T-testimony*

I. _____ _____

II. _____ _____

III. _____ _____

IV. _____ _____

_____ Speaker maintained strong eye contact

_____ Speaker had sufficient vocal variety (not monotone)

_____ Speaker articulated words clearly (not too soft/fast)

_____ Speaker was conversational (did not read speech)

_____ Speaker seemed poised and confident

_____ Speaker used appropriate gestures/physical movement

_____ Speaker used proper language and grammar

_____ Conclusion reinforced the central idea

_____ Conclusion ended on a strong note

Overall evaluation   A   A-   B+   B   B-   C+   C   C-   D+   D   D-   F

Source: Adapted from Lucas, S.E. (1995). *The art of public speaking: Instructor's manual* (5th ed.). New York: McGraw-Hill

Critical Listening Activity

Name _____

1. Provide an honest evaluation of your primary strengths and weaknesses as a listener. What steps do you need to take to become a better listener? Be specific.

2. Select a lecture in one of your other classes. Examine what the lecturer does most effectively. Identify three things this speaker could do better to help students maintain interest in the lecture.

3. Are you an effective, critical listener? Watch the lead story on *60 minutes, Dateline, Primetime,* or *20/20* and answer the following questions.

Who was the interviewer?

Who was being interviewed?

What was the topic of the story?

What was the purpose for covering this story?

What were the interviewees' qualifications for speaking on this topic?

Identify at least two main points from this story.

How did this story influence you?

A Listening Checklist

Review the following checklist (before and after listening to a speech) to help you recall some of the suggestions offered to enhance your listening skills.

YES	NO	Do I know how I feel about this topic before the speaker begins?
YES	NO	Am I ready to change my mind on this topic?
YES	NO	Did I work hard enough at listening?
YES	NO	Do I need to expend more effort?
YES	NO	Did the details of the message interfere with the main point?
YES	NO	Was I able to visualize the ideas presented?
YES	NO	Did my notes really help me, or are they just notes?
YES	NO	Did I let any aspect of the message irritate me unduly?
YES	NO	Did anything in the speaker's appearance or manner unduly affect me?
YES	NO	Was I responding just because others in the audience responded the same way?
YES	NO	Did this speaker really interest me?

Bostrom, R.N. (1988). *Communicating in public: Speaking and listening.* Edina, MN: Burgess Publishing.

Looking at the Audience:
Considering Your Passengers

Topic Choice: Determining the Destination

Chapter 5 Review Questions

Name _____

Upon completion of reading these two chapters, answer the questions below. Be prepared to discuss your responses in class. Use your answers as a study guide for the final examination.

1. How does being other-oriented enhance communication effectiveness? Provide an example. Most communicators can be grouped into three categories. What are they? Which of the three is most effective? Why?

2. What are the common audience characteristics that speakers should know about and take into consideration each time they begin speech preparation. Specify ways in which gender, age, educational level, economic status, ethnic or cultural background can affect the acceptance of a speaker's message.

3. Identify specific ways psychological and situational information can affect the acceptance of a specific message.

Chapter 6 Review Questions

4. Describe the process of invention. In your description focus on the ways in which invention is relevant to preparing a speech. What are the potential sources from which a speaker can select to identify a speech topic?

5. What are the four traditional speech purposes? Provide a definition of each purpose. What would be an example of a speech that matched the definition of each traditional speech purpose?

6. Define the following terms: central idea, general purpose, specific purpose? How can a speaker narrow a topic down to a specific purpose?

Audience Analysis: Gathering and Interpreting Information

Demographic Information

Use the following questions to assemble information about your classroom audience. Answer items one through nine to be handed in to your instructor. Your instructor can calculate simple percentages which will be extremely informative.

_____ 1. What is your sex?

    A.   Female
    B.   Male

_____ 2. What is your approximate age?

    A.   18-21
    B.   22-29
    C.   30-39
    D.   Over 40

_____ 3. What is your religious preference or background?

    A.   Catholic
    B.   Protestant
    C.   Jewish
    D.   Islamic
    E.   Other _____ (please indicate)

_____ 4. What is your primary co-cultural background?

    A.   Euroamerican
    B.   Latino, Hispanic, Mexican American
    C.   Native American
    D.   Asian American
    E.   African American
    F.   Middle Eastern American
    G.   Other _____ (please indicate)

_____ 5. What is your educational background (indicate the highest degree earned)?

    A.   Doctorate
    B.   Master's
    C.   Bachelor's
    D.   Associate degree
    E.   High school diploma
    F.   Other_____ (please indicate)

_____ 6. What is your economic status or annual salary (or, if still a dependent, your parents' economic background)?

    A.   Below $10,000
    B.   Between $10,000 and $20,000
    C.   Between $20,000 and $50,000
    D.   Between $50,000 and $100,000
    E.   Over $100,000

_____ 7. What is your current marital status?

    A.   Married
    B.   Single
    C.   Divorced

_____ 8. How many children do you have?

    A.   None
    B.   1
    C.   2 or 3
    D.   4 or more

_____ 9. Where do you live?

    A.   My parents' home
    B.   My own apartment or house
    C.   A dormitory
    D.   A fraternity or sorority
    E.   Other _____

Psychographic Information

Questions ten through thirteen can be copied and handed out to the members of your audience for each speech you present to the class. Upon collecting the completed items, calculate the mean, or average, audience score by summing up the responses for each item and then dividing by the number of completed responses. Upon obtaining mean scores (or percentages) for each question, you will have an idea as to how to write and present your speech.

_____ 10. To what extent are you liberal or conservative in your political orientation: (Circle the number that most closely reflects your attitude).

Liberal 5 4 3 2 1 Conservative

_____ 11. How involved are you on _____ (insert the topic of your presentation)?

Highly Involved 5 4 3 2 1 Uninvolved

_____ 12. How informed do you consider yourself to be on _____ (insert the topic of your presentation)?

Highly Informed 5 4 3 2 1 Uninformed

_____ 13. How interested are you in _____ (insert the topic of your presentation)?

Very Interested 5 4 3 2 1 Not at all interested

Adapted from Kearney, P., & Plax, T.G. (1996). *Public Speaking in a Diverse Society*. Mountain View, CA: Mayfield Publishing Company.

Brainstorming Utilizing
Categories Activity

Name _____

Brainstorming is a helpful means for generating speech topic ideas. Although some students prefer to brainstorm in a completely open manner, others find it effective to use a category system to direct their thinking. Below is a *sample* of brainstorming by using categories. After reviewing the sample, complete your own brainstorming on the following page.

Brainstorming Utilizing Categories
(sample)

Hobbies/interests

swimming

skiing

karate

reading

Places lived/traveled

South Carolina

Michigan

visit to Thailand

visit to Vermont

Major co-cultural affiliations

Irish/Italian

male

college student

son/brother

athlete

Democrat

Interesting personal experiences

survived tornado

saved a drowning child

volunteered at *Habitat for Humanity*

mother grew up with David Letterman

Issues of interest

gun control

child abuse and neglect

recycling

drunk driving

Affirmative action

smoking in public places

Special skills, career and concern goals, areas of study

Communication Systems Management Major

good at computers

taught skiing and snowboarding

goal: work for MCI

Brainstorming Utilizing Categories

Hobbies/interests

Places lived/traveled

**Major co-cultural
affiliations**

**Interesting personal
experiences**

**Issues of interest
and concern**

**Special skills, career
goals, areas of study**

Design a Speech Topic Purpose

Group Members Names: _____

Below are 20 topics. Select any three (or choose your own) and for each of the three compose a specific purpose statement and central idea appropriate for an informative speech. Now, using the *same* topics, develop a specific purpose statement and central idea appropriate for a persuasive speech. Next, evaluate the suitableness of the topics for your audience.

Dorm food	Steroids
Dieting	Child Abuse/Neglect
Fraternity/Sorority Life	Alcoholism
Single Parents	The Internet
Censorship	Divorce
Sexually Transmitted Diseases	Suicide
Insanity Plea in Court	Gun Control
Affirmative Action	Date Rape
Preparing for a Wedding	Homelessness
Legalization of Marijuana	Television

Topic #1 _____

General Purpose: To Inform

Specific Purpose:

Central Idea:

Topic #1 _____

General Purpose: To Persuade

Specific Purpose:

Central Idea:

Topic #2 _____

General Purpose: To Inform

Specific Purpose:

Central Idea:

Topic #2 _____

General Purpose: To Persuade

Specific Purpose:

Central Idea:

Topic #3 _____

General Purpose: To Inform

Specific Purpose:

Central Idea:

Topic #3 _____

General Purpose: To Persuade

Specific Purpose:

Central Idea:

Developing Content and Materials:

Choosing the Route

Chapter 7 Review Questions

Name _____

Upon completion of reading this chapter, answer the questions below. Be prepared to discuss your responses in class. Use your answers as a study guide for the final examination.

1. In what ways can first-hand experience be integrated into a speech? How can current events, interviews, and library sources be integrated into a speech?

2. How can you use online resources to accumulate information for a speech? How should you use keywords to narrow your search of online resources? What types of information and resources can be derived from NOTIS OPAC and the Academic Index?

3. What are the different types of examples that can be used for a speech? Provide an example of each type. How are illustrations different from examples?

4. Why can definitions be helpful for audience members listening to a speech? Provide an example of how a definition could be integrated appropriately into a presentation.

5. Under what circumstances would a speaker want to present comparisons or contrasts to audience members? Provide an example of a comparison or contrast that might be helpful for you in giving a speech on a particular topic.

6. Imagine that you have acquired all of the potential research material useful for a specific speech. How do you go about making choices about which research material to include and which to discard (or save for later use)?

Library Activity

Name _____

Using the library and/or the world wide web, answer the following questions. Identify the correct answer and your source. Each student may be assigned one question to answer; or, the questions may be divided up among students to work in pairs or groups.

1. Who was the first woman to fly alone around the world? When did this famous event occur? When was she born and where? What was her nickname?

2. How would you define *ESCHATOLOGY*? How would you use this word in a sentence?

3. What important event occurred on January 28, 1986? Where did this incidence transpire and why? Who was most affected?

4. What year did Joan Lunden join the staff of the *Good Morning America* show on ABC-TV? What was here name before she changed it to Joan Lunden?

5. Who was Meindert Hobbema? What type of art did this person do? During what period of time did this individual live and where?

6. On September 5, 1989, Chris Evert played her last match at the U.S. Open. Who did Chris Evert play and who won the match?

7. What is the definition of *NEONATE*? How would you use this word in a sentence?

8. *L'Histoire de Babar* (The Story of Babar), the first of a popular series of children's books featuring Babar the Elephant, is published. Identify the year and the author.

9. Who was the youngest President of the United States? What age was he? Who was the oldest man to become President of the United States? What age was he?

10. Who was the first black female millionaire in the United States? When and where was she born? Where did she live when she became a millionaire and how did she become one?

11. When and where was Amelia Earhart born? In what year did she vanish over the Pacific Ocean? What were her greatest accomplishments?

12. What is a synonym for the word *RILL*? How would you use this word in a sentence?

13. What historical event(s) occurred on April 30, 1945?

14. Identify the federal law that was passed on October 31, 1978 that changed working women's lives forever.

15. Who founded the *Stepfamily Association of America?* What percentage of American children live in stepfamilies?

16. In 1995, who were the top 3 draft choices for the Cincinnati Bengals?

17. What is a *CHEVESAILE*? How would you use this word in a sentence?

18. Who achieved the first manned flight of a power-driven, heavier-than-air machine. When and where did this historic event occur?

19. Which President of the United States was never elected? How did this occur? How long did he serve as President of the United States?

20. Who was the first woman to win the Pulitzer Prize for international reporting? Explain how she earned this award?

21. In 1995, who were the Best Actor and Best Actress for both the Academy Awards and the Golden Globe Awards?

22. A *GAUMLESS* person is...

23. What famous concert occurred on July 13, 1985? Where was the concert located? Who organized the event? How much money was raised?

24. Where was the development of the first underground rapid transit system (subway). When did this historic event occur?

25. Who won the best record and who won the best album at the 1980 Grammy Awards?

26. In what year was the *Women's Rights National Historic Park* established? Where is the park located?

27. When, where, and why did American political activist Ethel Rosenberg die?

28. A *CAMELOPARD* is a facetious name for a _____.

29. The names of the days in English are *Sunday, Monday, Tuesday, Wednesday, Thursday, Friday, and Saturday*. What are the names of the days in Italian?

30. Who was the last Russian Tsar? What were the names of his wife and children? What historic event occurred in July 1918? Who was the family's unusual friend? Which daughter became a legend?

Useful Communication Bookmarks

Search Engines

MetaCrawler Searching
http://metacrawler.cs.washington.edu:
8080/index.html

HotBot
http://www.hotbot.com/

WebCrawler Searching
http://webcrawler.com/

Alta Vista: Main Page
http://altavista.digital.com/

Archie Request Form
http://hoohoo.ncsa.uiuc.edu/archie.html

Listing of Listservs Worldwide
http://www.tile.net/listserv/

FTP Interface
http://hoohoo.ncsa.uiuc.edu/ftp/

DisInformation
http://www.disinfo.com/

Electric Library
http://www.elibrary.com/id/2525/search.cgi

Dogpile
http://www.dogpile.com/

OpenText
http://index.opentext.net

Excite
http://www.excite.com/

Lycos
http://www.lycos.com/

Information Directories/Web Guides

Yahoo
http://www.yahoo.com/

Infoseek
http://guide.infoseek.com/
Home?page=Home.html&sv=N3"

Web Ring Directory
http://www.webring.com/

INTERNET - Directories
http://www.december.com/cmc/info/
internet-directories.html

Look Smart
http://www.looksmart.com/x02/

CNET SEARCH.COM
http://www.search.com/?nscp

SEARCH.COM - desperately seeking someone
you know
http://www.search.com/Seeking/Someone/

Switchboard - Search for People's Phone
Numbers
http://www2.switchboard.com/

Webcrawler
http://www.webcrawler.com

Galaxy
http://galaxy.einet.net

Journalists' Source List
http://www.mediasource.com/Links.html

General Reference

Internet Public Library
http://ipl.sils.umich.edu/

The Skeptic's Dictionary
http://wheel.ucdavis.edu/-btcarrol/skeptic/
dictcont.htme

Speechwriters Bookshelf
gopher://gopher.arcade.uiowa.edu:2270/OF-
1%3a35095%3aSpeechwriters%20Bookshelf

Welcome to the Top of the Web
http://www.december.com/web/top.html

FAQ's by category
http://www.lib.ox.ac.uk/internet/news/faq/
by_category.index.html

Hypertext Webster's Dictionary
http://c.gp.cs.cmu.edu:5103/prog/webster

On-Line Reference works
http://www.cs.cmu.edu:8001/Web/
references.html

On-line Ready Reference
gopher://sol1.solinet.net/11/On-line Ready
Reference

Dictionaries etc
http://galaxy.einet.net/galaxy/Reference-
and-Interdisciplinary-Information/
Dictionaries-ect.html

Biographical Dictionary
http://www.mit.edu:8001/afs/athena/user/
g/a/galileo/Public/WWW/galileo.html

Barron's Guide to On-line Bibliographic
Databases
gopher://riceinfo.rice.edu/1ftp%3aftp.ut
dallas.edu%40/pub/staff/billy/libguide/

Virtual Law Library Reference Desk
http://lawlib.wuacc.edu/washlaw/reflaw/
reflaw.html

The World Wide Web Virtual Library
http://lcweb.loc.gov/

On-Line Reference Works
http://www.cs.cmu.edu/Web/
references.html

Webster's Dictionary
http://www.en.utexas.edu/
studentresources/referencedesk.html

Roget's Thesaurus of English Words and
Phrases
http://home.thesaurus.com/thesaurus/

The Virtual Institute of Information
http://www.ctr.columbia.edu/vi/

An Electronic Library of Classic Text
gopher://chico.rice.edu/11/Subject/
LitBooks

Dictionaries
http://galaxy.einet.net/galaxy/Reference-
and-Interdisciplinary-Information/
Dictionaries-etc.html

Reader's Guide
http://sawfish.lib.utexas.edu/~beth/Tour/
readersguide.html

All-in-One Site Improved
http://www.dreamscape.com/frankvad/
home.html

Metric Primer
http://www.dot.ca.gov/hq/oppd/metric/
metrictoc.html

Hypertext Webster Interface
http://c.gp.cs.cmu.edu:5103/prog/webster?

Biography Resources
http://www.tiac.net/users/parallax/

APPLICATIONS-Information-Library
http://www.december.com/cmc/info/
applications-information-library.html

APPLICATIONS-Communication-Mass
http://www.december.com/cmc/info/
applications-communication-mass.html

The Social Science Information Gateway
http://sosig.esrc.bris.ac.uk/

Internet Public Library
http://ipl.sils.umich.edu/

The World-Wide Web Virtual Library:
Statistics
http://stat.ufl.edu/vlib/statistics.html

My Virtual Reference Desk
http://www.refdesk.com/

Research It
http://www.iTools.com/research-it/

Background Briefing
http://www.backgroundbriefing.com/

In Reference
http://www.cs.uh.edu/~clifton/
macro.a.html

Project Gutenberg
http://www.promo.net/pg/

Communication Resources

Journal of Computer-Mediated
Communication
http://www.usc.edu/dept/annenberg/
journal.html

Communication Institute for on-line
scholarship
htt://WWW.CIOS.ORG/

Communication Scholars
http://alnilam.ucs.indiana.edu:1027/
sources/dirpage.html

CMC-Mass
http://www.december.com/net/tools/cmc-
mass.html

CMC Information Sources-Level 3 TOC
http://www.december.com/cmc/info/
toc3.html

ACA Social Science Communication Research
Collection
http://cavern. uark.edu/comminfo/www/
social.science.html

Media History Project
http://www.mediahistory.com/

Virtual Institute of Information
(telecommunications, mass media, and cyber
media)
http://www.ctr.columbia.edu/vi/
win_index.html

Film and Television Studies
http://eng.hss.cmu.edu/filmtv/

Media and Communication Studies
http://www.aber.ac.uk/~dgc/
medmenu.html

Communications Central
http://www.govst.edu/commcentral/

Academic Communication Sites Around the
World
http://www.jou.ufl.edu/commres/
jouwww.htm

American Communication Journal
http://www.uamont.edu/~adams/acj.html

Museum of Broadcast Communications
http://www.neog.com/mbc/

ERIC

ERIC (Educational Resources Information Center)
gopher://ericir.syr.edu/1

ERIC Clearinghouses (Syracuse)
gopher://ericir.syr.edu/11/Clearinghouses/16houses

ERIC/Reading, English, Communication
http://www.indiana.edu/~eric_rec/index.html

Quotations

Quotations
http://www.xmission.com:80/~mgm/quotes/

LoQtus Quotation Resource Page
http://pubweb.ucdavis.edu/Documents/Quotations/homepage.html

Bartlett, John. 1901. Familiar Quotations
http://www.columbia.edu/acis/bartleby/bartlett/

CHA's Quotations about change
http://www.cha4mot.com/quo_chng.html

CHA's Quotations about Communication
http://www.cha4mot.com/quo_comm.html

CHA's Quotations about ideas
http://www.cha4mot.com/quo_idea.html

CHA's Quotations about invention
http://www.cha4mot.com/quo_invt.html

CHA's Quotations about vocation
http://www.cha4mot.com/quo_voca.html

CHA's Quotations about life
http://www.cha4mot.com/quo_life.html

Style Sheets

APA Fequently Asked Questions
http://www.apa.org/journals/faq.html

Guide to Style Manuals
gopher://iliad.lib.duke.edu/00/DULib_Res/Bibliographies/STYLEMAN.HO

Network-Based Electronic Publishing of Scholarly Works
http://info.lib.uh.edu/pr/v6/n1/bail6n1.html

Basic Legal Citation
http://www.law.cornell.edu/citation/citation.table.html

The MLA-Style Citations
http://www.cas.usf.edu/english/walker/mla.html

Grammar and Style Notes
http://www.english.upenn.edu/~jlynch/grammar.html

Guide for Citing Electronic Information
http://www.wilpaterson.edu/wpcpages/library/citing.htm

Guide to Citing Govenment Information Sources
http://unr.edu/homepage/duncan/cite.html

MLA-Style Citations of Electronic Resources
http://www.cas.usf.edu/english/walker/mla.html

MLA Citation Guide
http://www.cas.usf.edu/english/walker/mla.html

MLA Guidelines to Evaluating Computer Related Work
http://jefferson.village.virginia.edu/mla.guidelines.html

Web Extension to APA style
http://www.nyu.edu/pages/psychology/WEAPAS

Web Extension to American Psychological Association Style
http://www.nyu.edu/pages/psychology/WEAPAS

Electronic Sources: MLA Style of Citation
http://www.uvm.edu/~xli/reference/
mla.html

Electronic Sources: APA Style of Citation
http://www.uvm.edu/~xli/reference/
apa.html

APA Publication Manual Crib Sheet
http://www.gasou.edu/psychweb/tipsheet/
apacrib.htm

Walker/ACW Style Sheet
http://www.cas.usf.edu/english/walker/
mla.html

Bibliographic Formats for Citing Electronic
Information
http://www.uvm.edu/~xli/reference/
estyles.html

Classroom Connect: REVISED How to Cite
Internet Resources (10/96)
http://www.classroom.net/classroom/
CitingNetResources.html

Copyright

Media and Telecommunications Policy and
Legislation, Copyright and Intellectual
Property Information
hhtp://www.lib.berkeley.edu/MRC/
MediaPolicy.html

Fair Use
http://www.libraries.psu.edu/avs/fairuse

The Copyright Website
http://www.benedict.com/

SUL: Copyright & Fair Use
http://fairuse.stanford.edu

Copyright management Center
http://gold.utsystem.edu./OGC/
IntellectualProperty/cprtindx.htm

ILTweb5:Projects:Copyright Guide:Index
http://www.ilt.columbia.edu/projects/
copyright/index.html

Bacal's Legal Sites
http://www.azlink.com/lawyers/

KuesterLaw Technology Law Resource-
Patent Copyright Trademark
http://www.kuesterlaw.com/index.html

Wellesley College Copyright Policy
http://www.wellesley.edu/Library/
copyright.html

Multimedia Product Dev.:Clearing Rights
http://www.batnet.com/oikoumene/
nobomediarights.html

Government Resources

Thomas-Legislative Information on the
Internet
http://thomas.loc.gov/

U.S.Government hypertexts
http://sunsite.unc.edu/govdocs.html

U.S. State Department
http://www.law.cornell.edu/

Federal Election Commission
http://www.fec.gov/

Federal Communications Commission
http://www.fcc.gov/

White House Briefing Room
http://www.whitehouse.gov/WH/html/
briefroom.html#fsbr

Office of the Director of Central Intelligence
http://www.odci.gov/

United States Postal service
gopher://www.usps.gov:80/hGET%20/

US Statistical Data
http://www.stat-usa.gov/

Government Statistics
http://www.fedstats.gov/

U.S. Government Printing Office
http://www.access.gpo.gov/

Statistical Abstract of the United States
http://www.census.gov/stat_abstract/

Smithsonian Institution
http://www.si.edu/

National Science Foundation
http://www.nsf.gov/

U.S. Government Documents and Publications
(NU)
gopher://toby.scott.nwu.edu/1D-
1%3a2652%3a04.fed.docs849289734 0 0

Federal Register (Counterpoint)
gopher://gopher.counterpoint.com/1

Factbook on Intelligence (CIA)
http://www.ic.gov/facttell/toc.html

United Nations Web Server
http://www.un.org/

U.N. Scholars Workstation
http://www.library.yale.edu/un/
unhome.htm

Related Organizations
http://www.unsystem.org/index.html

U.S. Postal Service
http://www.usps.gov

U.S. State Department's Travel Advisories
http://www.stolaf.edu/network/travel-
advisories.html

Tax Code Online
http://www.fourmilab.ch/ustax/ustax.html

Library of Congress Web
http://lcweb.loc.gov

IRS Digital Daily
http://www.irs.ustreas.gov/prod/
cover.html

Government Information
http://www.access.gpo.gov/su_docs/aces/
aces760.html

GPO Access
http://www.access.gpo.gov/su_docs/aces/
aaces002.html

Federal Budget
http://ibert.org

FedWorld
http://www.fedworld.gov/

PIPER Resources
http://www.piperinfo.com/~piper/state/
states.html

Local Government Web
http://www.localgov.org/

City.Net
http://www.city.net/countries/

Union of International
http://www.uia.org/website.htm

Federal Government Agencies
http://www.lib.lsu.edu/gov/fedgov.html

Communication Organizations

AEJMC
http://www.aejmc.sc.edu/online/home.html

Radio and Television News Directors
Foundation
http://www.rtndf.org/

American Association of Public Opinion
Research
http://www.aapor.org./

Broadcast Education Association
http://www.usu.edu/~bea/

Society for Technical Communication
http://stc.org/

Encyclopedia of Associations
gopher://gopher.cic.net:2000/11/e-serials/
archive/alphabetic/e/eoa

Scholarly Societies An Electronic Guide
http://www.lib.uwaterloo.ca/society/
overview.html

Society of Professional Journalists
ftp://ftp.netcom.com/pub/spj/html/
spj.html

ICA Home Page
http://www.io.com/~icahdq/ica/ica.html

Speech Communication Association
http://www.scassn.org/

WSCA - Western States Communication
http://www.csufresno.edu/speechcomm/
wsca.htm

SSCA - Southern States Communication
http://www.uamont.edu/~adams/
ssca.htmlx

SCA Undergraduate Student Organization
Page
http://cotton.uamont.edu/~roiger/scaclub/
start.html

American Communication Association
WWW Archives
http://www.uark.edu/depts/comminfo/
www/

Legal/Law Resources

Findlaw Internet Legal Resource
http://www.findlaw.com/

Individual Rights in America
http://asa.ugl.lib.umich.edu/chdocs/rights/
Citizen.html

Criminal Law Links
http://dpa.state.ky.us/~rwheeler/

Cornell's Legal Information Institute
http://www.law.cornell.edu/

News and Current Events

New York Times
http://www.nytimes.com

Washington Post
http://www.washingtonpost.com

Editor and Publisher
http://www.mediainfo.com

Links to Newspapers and News Services
http://www.newslink.org

An Internet news service
http://www.newspage.com

USA Today
http://www.usatoday.com

Wall Street Journal
http://www.wsj.com

Christian Science Monitor
http://www.csmonito.com/

Online newspapers
http://marketplace.com/e-papers.list.www/
e-papers.home.page.html

C-SPAN Gopher
gopher://c-span.org

World News
gopher://gopher.nstn.ca/11/Cybrary/News/
news

VOA Current News
gopher://gopher.VOA.Gov/1/newswire

The Electronic Newstand
http://www.enews.com/

Radio Tower
http://www.radiotower.com

Newslink
http://www.newslink.org

Newspage
http://www.newspage.com

Reuters
http://www.reuters.com/

PBS Newshour
http://www1.pbs.org/newshour/

Microsoft Network
http://www.msnbc.com

Fox News
http://www.foxnews.com

Weather Channel
http://www.weather.com/

Court TV
http://www.courttv.com

Television and Radio Sites

Radio Stations
http://www.brsradio.com/stations/

TV Stations
http://tvnet.com/tv/us/stations5.html

National Public Radio
http://www.npr.org

Radiospace
http://www.radiospace.com/

CBS
http://www.cbs.com

ABC
http://www.abc.com

NBC
http://www.nbc.com

CNN
http://www.CNN.com/

C-SPAN
http://www.c-span.org

VOA
http://www.voa.gov

WB
http://www.tv.warnerbros.com/

UPN
http://www.upn.com/

ESPN
http://espnet.sportszone.com

FOX
http://www.foxnetwork.com

PBS
http://www.pbs.org

TV resources
http://www.ultimatetv.com/

Discovery Channel
http://www.discovery.com

Turner Networks
http://www.turner.com

First Amendment — Free Speech

Banned books On-Line
http://www.cs.cmu.edu/People/spok/
banned-books.html

MediaScope
http://www.mediascope.org/mediascope/

Media Watch Dog
http://theory.lcs.mit.edu/~mernst/media/

Project Censored
http://censored.sonoma.edu/
ProjectCensored/

Call Them On It (Telecommunications)
http://www.callthemonit.com/

Electronic Frontier Foundation
http://www.eff.org/

Center for Democracy and Technology
http://www.cdt.org/

ACLU
http://www.aclu.org/

Fairness and Accuracy in Reporting
http://www.fair.org/fair/

Free Speech Issues
http://www.xnet.com/~paigeone/noevil/
noevil.html

Freedom Forum First Amendment Center
http://www.fac.org/

General Internet Resources

Frequently Asked Questions

Index to FAQ sites-Good Resource!
http://ps.superb.net/FAQ/

Welcome Newbie
http://www.netwelcome.com/index.html

E-mail Resources

FAQ: Finding e-mail addresses
http://www.cis.ohio-state.edu/hypertext/
faq/usenet/finding-addresses/faq.html

Beginner's guide to effective e-mail
http://www.webfoot.com/advice/
email.top.html

Remailer Information
http://electron-rutgers.edu:80/~gambino/
anon_servers/anon.html

HTML Resources

Compendium of HTML Elements
http://www.synapse.net/~woodall/
html.htm

HTML Goodies
http://www.htmlgoodies.com/

Newsgroups and Listservs

Reference.Com
http://www.Reference.COM/

Liszt Mailing List Directory
http://liszt.com/

Tile.net (Listserv and Newsgroup Resources)
http://www.tile.net/

Usenet FAQ
http://www.ou.edu/research/electron/
internet/use-faq.htm

Organizing Materials:
Arranging the Trip

Audio and Visual Elements: Sights and Sounds

Chapter 8 Review Questions

Name _____

Upon completion of reading these two chapters, answer the questions below. Be prepared to discuss your responses in class. Use your answers as a study guide for the final examination.

1. Identify the rationales for organization. Provide an example for each, different from the text.

2. Distinguish among the types of organization: chronological, spatial, topical (see textbook), causal, and problem-solution (see workbook, this chapter). Provide a unique example for each.

3. Demonstrate the process of outlining. Explain how verbal transitions can assist the listener (see workbook, this chapter). Finally, construct a suitable introduction and a conclusion to a speech.

Chapter 9 Review Questions

4. Identify involuntary ways that humans attend to certain stimuli as opposed to others.

5. Address the benefits and drawbacks of using demonstration, chalkboards, flip charts, and diagrams.

6. Discuss the advantages and disadvantages of using audio-visual equipment: the public address system, audio tape, overhead projectors, the slide projector, videotape, and multimedia.

Additional Patterns for Types of Organization

Causal speeches are arranged using a cause-and-effect relationship between main points and the subject of the speech. This pattern demonstrates the relationship between certain events or why something happens or happened. You would select a causal pattern when you want to outline a situation, condition or action from its causes to its effects, or from its effects back to its causes. The two main points for causal speeches may be organized one of two ways:

1. cause   1.   effect
2. effect   2.   cause

For example, some individuals refuse to leave their homes because they have an inordinate fear of crossing open spaces. Their agoraphobia is the *cause* and their refusal to leave their homes is the *effect*.

Problem-Solution speeches begin by stating a particular problem or need and then offering a practical solution to that problem. The pattern is quite simple in that the speaker convinces the listeners that a particular problem exists and then tells them how the problem can be solved. Another variation would be a problem-cause-solution order. This would be a speech with three main points: first identify the problem, second analyze the causes of the problem, and third present a solution to the problem. Chapter 14 provides a sophisticated problem-solution format in Monroe's Motivated Sequence.

Transitions

Internal Summary

One distinctive type of transition is the internal summary. The internal summary summarizes your preceding point or points. In addition, the internal summary consolidates and restates your ideas, which can help your listeners remember your message.

Internal Preview

The internal preview lets the audience know what the you are going to discuss next.

Internal summaries and internal previews are especially useful in cause-effect and problem solution speeches. An internal summary indicates to your listeners that you have concluded your discussion of the causes or problem and the internal preview signals you are ready to move on to the effects or solution.

Consider the following:

(Transition: *So now we see what the problem is. We know...... We know.... Now, the question is....? Let me tell you about a solution....*)

Verbal Transitions: Connecting the Main Points

Certain standard words or phrases can be used to signal other varieties of speech transitions.

Transition words or phrases that:

point out time changes

after	only last week
at last	in the future
later	twenty years ago
afterward	until now
at the same time	before
while	as soon as

signal additional information

furthermore	just as important
moreover	not only
in addition	next
also	and
besides	likewise

indicate a comparison is imminent

similarly	like
analogous to	comparable to

suggest a contrast will follow

on the other hand	in spite of
unfortunately	in contrast
however	on the contrary
although	but
nevertheless	regardless
notwithstanding	nonetheless

signify a spatial relationship

in the distance	as we move west (east, north, south)

imply a cause-and-effect relationship

as a result	therefore
consequently	because

Source: Adapted from Grice, G.L. & Skinner, J.F. (1998). *Mastering public speaking*. Needham Heights, MA: Allyn & Bacon.
Adapted from Osborn M. & Osborn, S. (1991). *Public speaking*. Boston, MA: Houghton Mifflin Company

Writing Your Outline:
A Guide

Title: The title of the speech reflects the essence of the speaker's topic, generates interest, and entices the audience to listen. A good title will be brief, descriptive, and creative.

Specific Purpose Statement: The specific purpose is a precise statement (appropriately informative or persuasive) of what the speaker intends to achieve with the particular topic. The specific purpose should be appropriate for the audience's interests, knowledge, and beliefs (pp 77-81).

Central Idea: The central idea is a one-sentence synopsis of your speech which presents the essence of the message, controlling idea, or main argument of a speech. The central idea should be worded carefully because it is the primary focus of your speech; all of the main points in the body of the speech will support the central idea (pp 69 and 197).

The specific purpose and central idea are usually constructed after you have finished your initial research and while you decide your main points.

Introduction: The introduction captures the audience's attention, establishes credibility for the speaker, orients the audience to the topic, and provides a preview statement which identifies the main points to be discussed in the body of the speech. The preview statement is usually the last component of an introduction (pp 109-110).

Body: The body of the speech should be written and outlined first. In planning the body of your speech, first, select and state the main points. You must have at least two main points in the body of the speech and at least two pieces of support material for each main point; therefore, if there is a *I* there is a *II*, if there is an *A* there is a *B*, if there is a *1* there is a *2*. Remember, each main point in the speech should be clearly independent of the other main points and at the same time support your thesis statement. Second, determine the best order (chronological, spatial, topical, causal, problem-solution). Third, select and develop the evidence to support the main points: examples, statistics, quotations, etc. Remember to orally cite your evidence in your speech and outline. Finally, use transitions to help the listeners understand how ideas are related to one another. Transitions are connectives between major or minor ideas in a speech (pp. 102-109).

I.   Write a simple and complete sentence stating your first main point. Your main point must support your central idea.
   A.   Write a simple and complete sentence supporting (I).
      1.   cite evidence and source
      2.   cite evidence and source

   B.   Write another simple and complete sentence, parallel with (A) and supporting (I).
      1.   cite evidence and source
      2.   cite evidence and source

Transition: Write a verbal transition by using a few words to connect (I) and (II) (textbook: pp 108-109; workbook: this chapter).

II.   Write a simple and complete sentence stating your second main point. Your second main point must support your central idea and be parallel with (I).
   A.   Write a simple and complete sentence supporting (II).
      1.   cite evidence and source
      2.   cite evidence and source
      3.   cite evidence and source

   B.   Write a simple and complete sentence, parallel with (II A) and supporting (II).
      1.   cite evidence and source
      2.   cite evidence and source

   C.   Write a simple and complete sentence, parallel with (II A & B) and supporting (II).
      1.   cite evidence and source
      2.   cite evidence and source

Transition: Write a verbal transition by using a few words to connect (II) and (III) (textbook: pp 108-109; workbook: this chapter).

III.   Write a simple and complete sentence stating your third main point. Your third main point must support your central idea and be parallel with (I) and (II).
   A.   Write a simple and complete sentence supporting (III).
      1.   cite evidence and source
      2.   cite evidence and source

   B.   Write another simple and complete sentence, parallel with (III A) and supporting (III).
      1.   cite evidence and source
      2.   cite evidence and source

Conclusion: The conclusion should pull the speech together showing how you will signal the end, summarize your main points, and stress the importance of your topic through a closing statement (a clincher). The conclusion should leave a lasting impression in the minds of your audience (pp 110-111).

Bibliography: Using APA (American Psychological Association) style, place a list of cited sources, arranged alphabetically, at the end of your speech outline. Keep in mind that you will need at least three cited sources for your demonstration speech and at least five cited sources for all other speech assignments. The following represents samples of APA style for books, magazines, journal articles, and newspaper articles. The first sample depicts the basic APA format while the second source exemplifies documenting and citing online information. For more information on documenting and citing online information, review the following books by Courtright and Perse (1998) as well as Harnack and Kleppinger (1998).

Books or Documents

Courtright, J.A., & Perse, E.M. (1998). *The Mayfield quick guide to the internet for communication students*. Mountain View, CA: Mayfield Publishing Company.

Harnack, A., & Kleppinger, E. (1998). *Online! A reference guide to using internet sources*. New York, NY: St. Martin's Press. [On-line]. Available: http://www.smpcollege.com/online-4styles~help

Magazines Articles

Hoffer, R. (1995, August 21). Mickey Mantle: The legacy of the last great player on the last great team. *Sports Illustrated*, 18-30.

Geier, T. (1997, December 22). 1997 charity guide: Maximize your charitable donations. *U.S. News* [On-line magazine]. Retrieved April 10, 1998 from the World Wide Web: http://www.usnews.com/usnews/nycu/charhigh.html

Journal Articles

Papa, M.J., & Natalle, E.J. (1989). Gender, strategy selection and discussion satisfaction in interpersonal conflict. *Western Journal of Speech Communication, 53*, 260-272.

Parks, M.R. & Floyd, K. (1996). Making friends in cyberspace. *Journal of Computer-Mediated Communication* [On-line serial], *1*(4). Retrieved March 26, 1998 from the World Wide Web: http://www.usc.edu/dept/annenberg/vol1/issue4/parks.html

Newspaper Articles

Estrich, S. (1995, May 9). Counterpoints: An apt compromise on affirmative action. *USA Today*, p. 9A.

Hampson, R. (1998, April 10). generous winner inspires many *USA Today* [On-line newspaper]. Retrieved April 10, 1998 from the World Wide Web: http://www.usatoday. com/news/acovfri.html

Scramble Exercise

Name _____

This is an outline scramble exercise. The following list of sentences are the main points and subpoints of an outline. Rearrange these sentences in outline form so that they make sense.

1. To avoid a drunk drive, slow down until the driver pulls off the road.

2. The second most frequently-occurring accident is caused by tailgaters.

3. To correct these situations you should take the following precautions.

4. Over four thousand deaths occur each year on our nation's highways. ⊥

5. By trying to follow these guides while driving, drivers can make our highways safe and pleasant places to travel.

6. To eliminate unwanted tailgaters, pull onto the shoulder of the road and let the other driver pass.

7. The third cause of accidents is unsafe lane changes.

8. The first major cause of auto accidents involves drunk drivers.

9. There are three major causes of highway accidents.

10. To make lane changing safer, avoid driving in the inside fast lane, and always be alert to surrounding traffic.

Scramble Outline

I. _____

II. _____

    A. _____

    B. _____

    C. _____

III. _____

    A. _____

    B. _____

    C. _____

IV. _____

Outline a Speech

Objective:

You will learn to generate a brief outline. After completing this activity, you will be able to share your best example with the class.

Procedure:

Get into small groups of three or four. Select two topics from the following list and generate a brief outline for each. Upon selecting a topic, write out a specific purpose statement and a central thesis statement. Next, identify an organizational pattern to fit the topic and select two to five main points to fit that pattern. After completing your outlines, be prepared to share your best example with the class.

How to change a tire
Backpacking through Europe
Daytime talk shows
Funding AIDS research
Being a blood donor
Popular spectator sports
University professors
Internet censorship
Protecting children's rights
How to quit smoking
Solving the homeless problem
The United States judicial system
The best and worst movies of the year
How to lose weight permanently
Drug testing in the workplace
Capital punishment
Our next President of the United States
Unwanted telephone solicitations
Dorm food
Illiteracy in America

Discussion Questions:

Which speech topics seemed to be chosen the most? How were these topics addressed differently? What criteria did you use to select the organizational pattern? How did you select your main points? What types of support material would you utilize to strengthen your main points?

Materials Required:

None

Time:

Approximately 25 - 30 minutes

Using Visual Aids

Review this list of speech topics and consider how you might use visual aids for each one.

1. Instructing your class to perform CPR on a drowning victim

2. Informing your audience as to the number of men and women killed while serving in the United States Armed Services

3. Describing to your classmates the difference in expected life spans between various nations

4. Teaching a group of individuals how to explore the Internet

5. Describing to your audience a recent trip you took to Washington D.C.

6. Informing your listeners about the length of sentences given for certain crimes and the length of time that criminals actually serve for those crimes

7. Explaining to your classmates how to make a taco

8. Persuading your audience that more money should be spent on AIDS research.

Visual Aids Check Sheet

1. _____ Is everything large enough to be seen by all without straining?

2. _____ Is everything written or drawn short and simple? Did I use heavy print, bright colors, few lines, large letters?

3. _____ Will I need a pointer?

4. _____ Can I cover or put away aid before and after it is needed?

5. _____ Can I summarize after the aid is used?

6. _____ Did I practice with my materials at home and time them according to my speech?

7. _____ Can I hand out handouts *before* the speech?

8. _____ Will I have all materials with me at the time of the speech?

9. _____ Do I know how much time I will need for showing the aid or drawing?

10. _____ Do I know exactly when the aid will be needed?

11. _____ Will I need an assistant and have I planned for this in advance?

12. _____ Will I be able to make my aids useful in relation to my speech?

Weaver, R.L. (1993). *Skills for communicating effectively* (4th ed.). Dubuque, IA: Kendall/Hunt Publishing Company.

Language: The Vehicle for Your Trip

Delivery: Plans into Action

Chapter 10 Review Questions   Name _____

Upon completion of reading these two chapters, answer the questions below. Be prepared to discuss your responses in class. Use your answers as a study guide for the final examination.

1. What is the symbolic nature of language? How can words have multiple interpretations or meanings? Differentiate denotative and connotative meaning?

2. Why is grammar important? Provide examples of poor grammar you hear often.

3. Distinguish among the characteristics of language (precision, appropriateness, economy, and vividness).

Chapter 11 Review Questions

4. Define nonverbal communication. How are messages most often conveyed through nonverbal communication? What are the functions of nonverbal communication.

5. Describe the effective use of your body in speech delivery. Identify the ways you can merge these messages into your presentation. Describe the vocal characteristics available to a public speaker.

6. Differentiate between manuscript, memorized, impromptu, and extemporaneous speeches. Provide examples for each.

Bias Free Language Activity

Objective:

The goal of this activity is to become more sensitive to words that may be offensive to audience members. You should be able to identify politically correct alternatives for various words.

Procedure:

Divide into groups of three and four students. Read the list of words (see next page) and choose alternative words that show respect and acceptance for people of different co-cultures.

Discussion Questions:

How difficult was it to identify politically correct alternatives for the words presented? Can you see how these words may be offensive to certain groups of people? Why? Why not? Can the use of bias language lower your credibility with an audience? How? Can the use of bias language seriously damage the effectiveness of your speech? How? When have you been offended by a speaker using certain words? How did it make you feel? What alternative words could the speaker have chosen that would have been more appropriate?

Time Required:

Approximately 20 - 30 minutes.

Source:

Adapted from Kearney, P. & Plax, T.G. (1996). *Public speaking in a diverse society*. Mountain View, CA: Mayfield Publishing Company.

Bias Free Language Activity

housewife	congressman
weatherman	poor
spinster	unwed mother
homosexual	vagrant/bum
policeman	mailman
handicapped	paperboy
mother country	waitress
bridesmaid/best man	stewardess
old folks home	bellboy
night watchman	salesman
manpower	mankind
maternity leave	cameraman

Using Correct Grammar

Objective:

The goal for this activity is to learn the importance for using proper grammar. You will read a grammatically incorrect statement and correct the error.

Procedure:

Form into pairs or groups of three. Identify the grammatically incorrect statement and re-write the statement using proper grammar (see next page).

Discussion Questions:

Was it difficult to identify why the statement was grammatically incorrect? Was correcting the grammatical error fairly simple? Why do people use incorrect grammar? When people use incorrect grammar regularly, how are they perceived by others? Why? How can poor grammar damage a person's career? How can poor grammar be detrimental for a person giving a public speech? How can you ensure you are using proper grammar in your speech?

Time Required:

Approximately 15 to 20 minutes

Source:

Adapted from Gregory, H. (1987). *Public speaking for college and career.* New York: Random House.

Incorrect	Correct
She don't	
You done it	
He had went	
I been thinking	
hisself	
I seen it	
Him and me went	
She come to see you yesterday	
He be late	
Give me them shoes	
You was	
Between you and I	
She's already went	
I've already took Public Speaking	
theirself	
Her and me went	
He ain't here	
She be late	
He had wrote it	
She don't love me no more	

Delivery Analysis

Objective:

To develop skills in analyzing the delivery of a speech.

Procedure:

Divide into groups of three or four. Your instructor will show a videotape of a person delivering a speech. While watching the videotape of this speech, focus on the aspects of delivery identified on your Delivery Analysis Form. Evaluate the speaker's delivery by offering specific comments about his or her performance (e.g., "The speaker established eye contact by looking directly at each member of the audience"). These comments can be written on the *Delivery Analysis Form* while the speaker is giving the presentation.

After the speech has ended write your final observations about the speaker's delivery.

Each group member should talk about their observations regarding the speaker's delivery. The purpose of this conversation is to produce one overall summary evaluation of the speaker's performance that can be shared with the class.

Discussion Questions:

1. How did you evaluate this speaker's delivery in terms of *enunciation, volume, pitch, rate, fluency, use of pauses, rhythm, eye contact, facial expression, gestures, movement,* and *physical appearance*?

2. What were the strengths of this speaker's delivery? Provide specific examples.

3. Were here any aspects of this speaker's delivery that could be improved? Provide specific examples.

Materials Required:

Videotape of a speech, and the delivery analysis form.

Time Required:

Ten to fifteen minutes to show the speech, fifteen minutes for in-group discussion, and fifteen minutes for group presentations focusing on the speaker's delivery.

Delivery Analysis Form

Instructions: You are about to view a videotape of a person delivering a speech. Focus on the aspects of delivery identified on this form. Offer specific statements to describe components of the speaker's delivery (e.g., "The speaker varied his volume and pitch in ways that gave a conversational tone to his delivery").

1. **Enunciation:** Did the speaker clearly pronounce words? Were there any obvious pronunciation or articulation mistakes?

2. **Volume:** Did the speaker speak loudly enough to be heard? Did the speaker vary his or her volume?

3. **Pitch:** Did the speaker speak at an appropriate pitch level? Did he or she change the pitch of his or her voice during the presentation?

4. **Rate:** Did the speaker speak too quickly or too slowly at any point in the speech? Did the speaker vary his or her speaking rate during the presentation?

5. **Pause:** Did the speaker incorporate pauses into his or her presentation? Was pausing used effectively throughout the speech?

6. **Rhythm:** How would you describe the rhythm or tempo of this speech?

7. **Fluency:** Was this a fluent presentation? Would you describe this as a smooth delivery? Did words flow freely and was there an absence of unnecessary pauses?

8. **Gestures:** Did the speaker effectively use gestures in this speech? List specific examples of gestures that were used effectively. Were any gestures used inappropriately?

9. **Movement:** Did the speaker stay in one place while speaking or did the speaker move away from one centralized location? Was the use of movement (or the lack of it) appropriate for this presentation?

10. **Eye Contact:** Did the speaker seem to establish eye contact with audience members? How did he or she accomplish this? (If this speaker was required to look only at a camera, did they maintain eye contact with the camera?)

11. **Facial Expression:** Were the speaker's facial expressions consistent with the message he or she was trying to send? Did the speaker communicate with his or her audience through facial expression? How?

12. **Physical Appearance:** Was the speaker's physical appearance appropriate for the occasion? Were there any aspects of the speaker's physical appearance that you feel are important to comment upon?

Informative Speaking:

Special Precautions

Chapter 12 Review Questions   Name _____

Upon completion of reading this chapter, answer the questions below. Be prepared to discuss your responses in class. Use your answers as a study guide for the final examination.

1. Define information according to our text: general and specific.

2. Characterize how the relaying function operates in informative speaking.

3. What is the difference between informative speeches that relay and those that externalize?

4. Percepts and schemas are related to the development of new information. Explain how.

5. Describe the four major types of informative speaking. How are they different?

6. Topical, spatial and chronological organizational patterns can be used in informative speaking. Describe how each of these patterns can be used in an informative speech.

Develop an Informative Speech Topic

Objective:

The goal of this activity is to learn to write a specific purpose statement for an informative speech.

Procedure:

Divide yourselves into pairs or groups of three people. Select four of the topics and formulate a specific purpose statement for an informative speech for each of the four. The four specific purpose statements must include one topic for a speech of demonstration, one topic for a speech of explanation or briefing, one topic for a speech of self-description and one topic for a speech of statistical information. If you do not like any of the suggestions below, feel free to choose your own. Finally, select the best organizational pattern for presenting your informative speech topic.

cameras	domestic violence
internet	tornados
hand guns	voting
vegetarian	yoga
comic strips	Leonardo DiCaprio
kleptomania	tourism
child abuse	Vietnam War
Nelson Mandela	capital punishment
subways	Grand Canyon
racial discrimination	hanging wallpaper

Discussion Questions:

How did you differentiate between the speech of demonstration, speech of explanation, speech of self-description and the presentation of statistical information? Which pattern did you choose for each? Why? Which topics would make the most interesting informative speeches? What other topics do you find interesting for informative speaking?

Materials Required:

Developing Topics for Informative Speeches handout (next page)

Time Required:

Approximately 30 to 40 minutes

Source:

Adapted from Lucas, S.E. (1983). *The art of public speaking: Instructor's manual* (3rd ed.). New York: Random House.

Developing Topics for Informative Speeches

Speech of Definition

Topic:
Specific Purpose:

Pattern: Chronological   Spatial   Topical
(circle one)

Speech of Description

Topic:
Specific Purpose:

Pattern: Chronological   Spatial   Topical
(circle one)

Speech of Explanation

Topic:
Specific Purpose:

Pattern: Chronological   Spatial   Topical
(circle one)

Speech of Demonstration

Topic:
Specific Purpose:

Pattern: Chronological   Spatial   Topical
(circle one)

Create a Speech of Explanation

Objective:

The purpose for this activity is to understand the complexity of giving information to an audience who is unfamiliar with the topic. Your goal is to learn to organize and present a speech of explanation.

Procedure:

Divide into groups of three and four students. Each group will select one of the topics listed below (or a unique topic of their choice). Each group has approximately 15 minutes to create a two-minute speech of explanation. The speech is designed for an audience who knows NOTHING about the topic presented. The speech may be presented by one member of the group or the speech may be divided up and presented by the entire group.

How to write a poem
How to change a light bulb
Hosting a dinner party
Doing laundry at college
Writing a resume
Cheating at cards
How to dress for less
Playing tennis
Making great coffee
Choosing a college
Surviving finals week

Discussion Questions:

How difficult was it to design a speech for a group of listeners who are totally unfamiliar with your topic. Did you include all of the details necessary to properly explain your topic? Why? Why not? Which one of the speeches presented today did you like best? Why? What could your group have done to explain your topic better? What implications does this have for your informative speaking in the future?

Materials Required:

Create a Speech of Explanation handout (next page)

Time Required:

Approximately 35 to 40 minutes

Source:

Adapted from Lucas, S.E. (1995). *The art of public speaking: Instructor's manual* (5th ed.). New York: McGraw-Hill.

Create a Speech of Explanation Outline

Topic:

Specific Purpose:

Central Idea:

Introduction:

Body:

Conclusion:

Persuasive Speaking:

Navigating the Territory

Chapter 13 Review Questions

Name _____

Upon completion of reading this chapter, answer the questions below. Be prepared to discuss your responses in class. Use your answers as a study guide for the final examination.

1. In terms of their communication function, illustrate the uniqueness of informative and persuasive speaking. Discuss the difference between speeches that change, reinforce, and shape responses.

2. Explain the process in which changing an individual's attitudes can actually influence his or her potential behavior.

3. Address how cognitive consistency operates in persuasive speeches. Provide a unique example.

4. Differentiate between the peripheral and central processing route. What are the practical difficulties for each.

5. Identify the four characteristics of credibility. In your opinion, which of the four is most important and why.

6. How can you work on elements in your message and presentation to enhance your chances of credibility. When have you been affected by a persuasive speech?

Create a Plan

Name _____

1. Create a plan for how you want to be perceived by your audience. Visualize the image or impression you want to create. Identify nonverbal and verbal strategies that will help you communicate that impression to your audience.

2. List all the common ground you share with most of the people in your audience. How can you use this list to try to establish common ground with your audience?

3. How can you make your speech worth listening to? How can you make your speech memorable? Dynamism helps you hold your audience's attention. What are some ways you can add dynamism to your speech delivery?

4. It is important that you appear trustworthy to your audience. How do you plan to build the audience's trust in you?

5. How can you exhibit competence in your speech? How can you communicate your competence without seeming arrogant?

6. As an ethical speaker, it is important that you say what you truly believe, not just what the audience wants to hear. How do you plan to be an ethical speaker.

You're the Instructor:
An Ethics Activity

Name _____

You are the instructor for the Introduction to Public Speaking Course. Read the following scenarios and determine the following:

1. Whether or not the speech/topic or delivery is ethically appropriate for the classroom.

2. How the student can deliver the topic in the most ethical manner.

In answering these questions, you should list the issues to be considered and how you will handle them.

Scenarios

1. A speaker plans to do a persuasive speech on the music industry. She plans to show rock and rap videos that have obscene and graphic language.

2. A speaker, who is Neo-Nazi, wants to do a persuasive speech praising Adolf Hitler.

3. A speaker is scheduled to give a persuasive speech on pornography. When it is time for this student to present, the speaker brings out sexually explicit visual aids to illustrate the main points and proceeds to show the materials during the speech.

4. A speaker gave a speech on cults and described the Branch Davidians in detail, claiming to have been a member for 2 years. After the speech, you hear her bragging to a friend that she was never in the cult and only used that example for effect.

You're Opposed to the Topic: An Adaptation Activity

Name _____

1. Identify a topic for which you have strong feelings and opinions (e.g., abortion, politics, current events, gun control, religious beliefs, cultural practices, violence on television, etc.). Briefly describe your opinion on this topic.

2. Place yourself in a situation in which you are to listen to a speaker who opposes your position on the issued identified above. How should this speaker adapt his or her presentation to not offend audience members who hold positions similar to yours (without requiring the speaker to change his or her position on this issue). What types of arguments, evidence, or ideas could this speaker present to cause you to question the strength of your position on this topic?

Finding Persuasive Message Strategies:

The "Rules" of the Road

Chapter 14 Review Questions

Name _____

Upon completion of reading this chapter, answer the questions below. Be prepared to discuss your responses in class. Use your answers as a study guide for the final examination.

1. Define each of the essential elements in the Toulmin model of reasoning: claim, data, warrant, backing, qualifier, and reservation.

2. What is an argument field? Provide a unique example.

3. Explain the five steps in Monroe's Motivated sequence.

4. Develop a unique example for the specific steps in Monroe's Motivated Sequence: attention, need, satisfaction, visualization, and action.

5. Describe other approaches that can be used to develop persuasive messages.

6. Provide a unique example of a strategy for overcoming apathy or a strategy for overcoming audience disbelief.

Toulmin's Model of Reasoning
Activity

Name_____

The focus of Toulmin's Model of Reasoning is on the claim which is what the speaker asks the receiver to accept or believe or do. What claims would you make for the following situations? What are the particular beliefs that must be held by the receiver (data) for the claim to be accepted? What is the general belief (warrant) that allows for the acceptability of the claim based on the relevant data.

1. You have been pulled over by a police officer for driving 5 miles over the speed limit. You want to convince the officer not to issue you a ticket.

2. You have volunteered for your favorite non-profit organization, *The American Cancer Society*. You want to solicit donations from the people in your community.

3. You purchased a product and you are extremely dissatisfied. You return the product to the store and you are seeking a full refund.

4. You are attracted to a person in this class and you would like to take the relationship further. You want to ask this special someone out for a date.

5. You have received your final grade in this public speaking class and the grade is lower than what you expected. You want to request a grade change from your instructor.

Monroe's Motivated Sequence

Scramble Exercise

Read the following list of sentences based on a speech about the need for better health care. Rearrange these sentences to fit Monroe's Motivated Sequence.

1. The United States would join nations like Canada, where no one fears seeing a doctor because of cost.

2. You could become one of 37 million uninsured Americans who face financial ruin if they become seriously ill.

3. Write your senator and representative today, urging the passage of national health insurance.

4. A child dies because her parents couldn't afford to take her to the doctor.

5. National health insurance would guarantee all Americans the right to health care, regardless of their income.

I. *Attention:*

II. *Need:*

III. *Satisfaction:*

IV. *Visualization:*

V. *Action:*

Source: Brydon, S.R. & Scott, M.D. (1994). *Between one and many: The art and science of public speaking*. Mountain View, CA: Mayfield Publishing Company.

Sample Final Exam Questions

1. According to our textbook, the _____ is one factor that distinguishes interpersonal communication from public speaking.

    a. nonverbal message
    b. internal noise
    c. nature of the message
    d. feedback from the receivers

2. A critical component in persuasive speaking is how the speaker is perceived by the audience. Which term BEST identifies this component?

    a. charisma
    b. power
    c. poise
    d. credibility

3. "To inform my audience about the six warning signals for cancer" is an example of a(n) _____for an informative speech.

    a. specific purpose
    b. central idea
    c. transition
    d. title

4. A speech in which the outline is carefully prepared, but the exact words are not chosen in advance is called a(n)_____ speech.

    a. impromptu
    b. manuscript
    c. extemporaneous
    d. memorized

5. According to our textbook, saying "She done it" instead of "She did it" is an error in

    a. articulation
    b. grammar
    c. precision
    d. vividness

Answers for sample final exam questions 1-5

1. c (see chapter 1, page 5)

2. d (see chapter 13, page 171)

3. a (see chapter 6, pages 77-78)

4. c (see chapter 11, page 148)

5. b (see chapter 10, page 129)

6. All of the following are necessary in a speech outline *except*

   a. a consistent pattern of indentation
   b. directions for delivering the speech
   c. transitions
   d. coordination and subordination

7. _____ are clear sheets of acetate that can be created with a copy machine or drawn on with an erasable marker.

   a. Slides
   b. Computer-generated graphics
   c. Transparencies
   d. Diagrams

8. What is the *first* step in Monroe's motivated sequence?

   a. satisfaction
   b. need
   c. visualization
   d. attention

9. When you listen to evaluate arguments, message strategies, and other components of effective speaking, what kind of listening is involved?

   a. reflective
   b. comprehensive
   c. empathic
   d. critical

10. Ben has waited until the last minute to prepare his speech for his public speaking class. Desperate, Ben pulled a speech outline from his fraternity's files and used it for his assignment. According to our text, Ben has relegated to which of the following choices?

    a. plagiarism
    b. seducer communicator
    c. faulty accountability
    d. unscrupulous intent

Answers for sample final exam questions 6-10

6.   b (see chapter 8, pages 107-109)

7.   c (see chapter 9, page 121)

8.   d (see chapter 14, page 184)

9.   d (see chapter 15, pages 196-197 and 199)

10.   a (see chapter 3, pages 39-41)

SPEECH #1

1. Speech Topic Evaluation Form

2. Demonstration Speech Evaluation Form

3. Outline Evaluation Form

4. Self-Analysis of Speech Evaluation

Speech Topic Evaluation Form

Name——————————————————   Topic Idea ——————————————————

All students must have their topic approved at least one week prior to speaking.

—————— Do you have an interest and/or knowledge in the topic?

—————— If not, do you have a sincere interest in learning more about it? How do you plan to research your topic?

—————— Will the topic interest your audience? If the topic is interesting to you but may not interest your audience, how can you arouse their interest in your topic?

—————— Is your audience already familiar with this topic? If so, how can you present new information about this topic to your audience?

—————— Is your topic ethically appropriate?

—————— Does the topic improve our people and our society? How?

—————— Is the topic appropriate for the assignment?

—————— Is the topic of significance to your classmates?

—————— Is the topic timely and connected to current concerns?

—————— Is the speech tailored to meet the time allocated for the assignment?

—————— Could the speech be narrowed? How?

Provide a tentative outline for your speech. Include ideas for a specific purpose, central idea, attention getter in introduction, main points, support material, visual aids, and a clincher in closing.

Demonstration Speech Evaluation Form

Speaker_____   Topic _____

+ excellent   ✔ competent   - needs improvement

Content

_____ There is a clear specific purpose applicable to the audience

_____ The speech is adapted to the audience's interests, knowledge, and attitudes

_____ The members of the audience learned how to do something or how something works

Organization

_____ The introduction gains attention, relates topic to audience, establishes credibility, previews body of the speech

_____ Organization of speech is obvious and appropriate

_____ The main points of the speech are clearly stated, they follow a logical pattern

_____ The conclusion related back to the introduction. It was dynamic!

Presentational Aid

_____ The presentational aid can be seen by everyone

_____ The presentational aid relates to the topic, situation, and audience

_____ The presentational aid helped to get the speaker's message across

_____ Rehearsed the use of the visual aid adequately (visual aid use goes smoothly, not distracting)

_____ Uses visual aid in a manner consistent with time limits (did dealing with visual aid extend the speaking time or use up time during which the speaker should have been speaking?)

Delivery

_____ Establishes audience contact (eye contact, distance)

_____ Voice quality (not monotone, too soft, too fast, etc.)

_____ Used appropriate language and grammar

_____ Delivery is extemporaneous (conversational, did not read speech)

_____ Freedom from distractions (swaying, fidgeting, "um")

_____ Appropriate use of gestures and physical movement

Topic Selection and Time Requirement

_____ Topic is sufficiently narrowed and focused

_____ Observes time limit

Outline Evaluation Form

Attach the following checklist to your speech outline

Speaker _____   Topic _____

+ excellent   ✔ competent   - needs improvement

Title

_____ reflects the topic and generates interest

Specific Purpose

_____ is an infinitive phrase that expresses the intention of the speaker in terms of the audience

_____ is realistic and appropriate for the audience's interests, average knowledge level, and beliefs

Central Idea

_____ is a single, unambiguous sentence that expresses the central argument or idea that the speaker will develop

_____ makes a clear factual claim, is narrow, and is not vague

Introduction

_____ includes an attention getting statement

_____ establishes credibility

_____ links the topic to the audience

_____ previews the main ideas of the speech

Body

_____ follows the rules of formal outlining throughout, indenting correctly and using appropriate numbers and letters

_____ the main points provide logical and compelling support that further the central idea

the subpoints represent well thought out examples, reasons, or arguments, accompanied by
_____ a cited source

Transitions

_____ located between the introduction and main body, between each main point of the speech, and between the body of the speech and its conclusion

Conclusion

_____ signals the end

_____ reaffirms your main points

_____ stresses the importance of your topic through a final statement (a clincher) that leaves a lasting impression in the minds of your listeners

Bibliography

_____ lists all sources cited in the body of the outline

_____ contains the required number of sources using APA format

Grammar

_____ complete sentences were used throughout the outline

_____ punctuation was accurate and all words were spelled correctly

Self-Analysis of Speech Evaluation

Name_____ Date _____

Speech Topic _____

Write a self-evaluation of the speech you have just given in class. Make sure your evaluation is objective and that it represents your true feelings about your performance. In the space provided make a list of strong and weak points you noticed in your speech.

Personal Evaluation of Speech

Strong Points	Weak Points
1.	1.
2.	2.
3.	3.
4.	4.
5.	5.

In a brief paragraph describe specific problems you encountered in your speech and suggest ways these problems might have been avoided or solved.

As a result of your instructor evaluation, peer evaluation, and self evaluation, list several positive steps you plan to take in your next speech to improve your communication evaluation.

SPEECH #2

1. Speech Topic Evaluation Form

2. Speech Evaluation Form

3. Outline Evaluation Form

4. Self-Analysis of Speech Evaluation

Speech Topic Evaluation Form

Name_____   Topic Idea _____

All students must have their topic approved at least one week prior to speaking.

_____ Do you have an interest and/or knowledge in the topic?

_____ If not, do you have a sincere interest in learning more about it? How do you plan to research your topic?

_____ Will the topic interest your audience? If the topic is interesting to you but may not interest your audience, how can you arouse their interest in your topic?

_____ Is your audience already familiar with this topic? If so, how can you present new information about this topic to your audience?

_____ Is your topic ethically appropriate?

_____ Does the topic improve our people and our society? How?

_____ Is the topic appropriate for the assignment?

_____ Is the topic of significance to your classmates?

_____ Is the topic timely and connected to current concerns?

_____ Is the speech tailored to meet the time allocated for the assignment?

_____ Could the speech be narrowed? How?

Provide a tentative outline for your speech. Include ideas for a specific purpose, central idea, attention getter in introduction, main points, support material, visual aids, and a clincher in closing.

Speech Evaluation Form

Speaker_____   Topic_____

+ excellent   ✔ **competent**   **- needs improvement**

Introduction

_____ Establishes favorable attention and interest

_____ Provides a clear specific purpose applicable to the audience

_____ Previews body of the speech

Content

_____ Speech is adapted to the audience's interests, knowledge, and attitudes

_____ Organization of speech is obvious and appropriate

_____ The main points are clearly identified

_____ Used appropriate transitions and internal summaries

_____ Evidence of research and support material (sources cited)

_____ Used acceptable logic, reasoning and emotional appeals

Delivery

_____ Establishes audience contact (eye contact, distance)

_____ Voice quality (not monotone, too soft, too fast, etc.)

_____ Used appropriate language and grammar

_____ Delivery is extemporaneous (conversational, did not read)

_____ Freedom from distractions (swaying, fidgeting, "um")

_____ Appropriate use of gestures, physical movement and visual aids

Conclusion

_____ Reminds audience of main points of speech

_____ Specifies precisely what the audience is to think or do in response to speech

_____ Ended strongly

Topic Selection and Time Requirement

_____ Topic is sufficiently narrowed and focused

_____ Observes time limit

Outline Evaluation Form

Attach the following checklist to your speech outline

Speaker _____   Topic _____

+ **excellent**   ✔ **competent**   - **needs improvement**

Title

_____ reflects the topic and generates interest

Specific Purpose

_____ is an infinitive phrase that expresses the intention of the speaker in terms of the audience

_____ is realistic and appropriate for the audience's interests, average knowledge level, and beliefs

Central Idea

_____ is a single, unambiguous sentence that expresses the central argument or idea that the speaker will develop

_____ makes a clear factual claim, is narrow, and is not vague

Introduction

_____ includes an attention getting statement

_____ establishes credibility

_____ links the topic to the audience

_____ previews the main ideas of the speech

Body

_____ follows the rules of formal outlining throughout, indenting correctly and using appropriate numbers and letters

_____ the main points provide logical and compelling support that further the central idea

_____ the subpoints represent well thought out examples, reasons, or arguments, accompanied by a cited source

Transitions

_____ located between the introduction and main body, between each main point of the speech, and between the body of the speech and its conclusion

Conclusion

_____ signals the end

_____ reaffirms your main points

_____ stresses the importance of your topic through a final statement (a clincher) that leaves a lasting impression in the minds of your listeners

Bibliography

_____ lists all sources cited in the body of the outline

_____ contains the required number of sources using APA format

Grammar

_____ complete sentences were used throughout the outline

_____ punctuation was accurate and all words were spelled correctly

Self-Analysis of Speech Evaluation

Name_____ Date _____

Speech Topic _____

Write a self-evaluation of the speech you have just given in class. Make sure your evaluation is objective and that it represents your true feelings about your performance. In the space provided make a list of strong and weak points you noticed in your speech.

Personal Evaluation of Speech

Strong Points	**Weak Points**
1.	1.
2.	2.
3.	3.
4.	4.
5.	5.

In a brief paragraph describe specific problems you encountered in your speech and suggest ways these problems might have been avoided or solved.

As a result of your instructor evaluation, peer evaluation, and self evaluation, list several positive steps you plan to take in your next speech to improve your communication evaluation.

SPEECH #3

1. Speech Topic Evaluation Form

2. Speech Evaluation Form

3. Outline Evaluation Form

4. Self-Analysis of Speech Evaluation

Speech Topic Evaluation Form

Name——————————————————————   Topic Idea ——————————————————————

All students must have their topic approved at least one week prior to speaking.

—————— Do you have an interest and/or knowledge in the topic?

—————— If not, do you have a sincere interest in learning more about it? How do you plan to research your topic?

—————— Will the topic interest your audience? If the topic is interesting to you but may not interest your audience, how can you arouse their interest in your topic?

—————— Is your audience already familiar with this topic? If so, how can you present new information about this topic to your audience?

—————— Is your topic ethically appropriate?

—————— Does the topic improve our people and our society? How?

—————— Is the topic appropriate for the assignment?

—————— Is the topic of significance to your classmates?

—————— Is the topic timely and connected to current concerns?

—————— Is the speech tailored to meet the time allocated for the assignment?

—————— Could the speech be narrowed? How?

Provide a tentative outline for your speech. Include ideas for a specific purpose, central idea, attention getter in introduction, main points, support material, visual aids, and a clincher in closing.

Speech Evaluation Form

Speaker_____   Topic _____

+ excellent   **✔ competent**   **- needs improvement**

Introduction

_____ Establishes favorable attention and interest

_____ Provides a clear specific purpose applicable to the audience

_____ Previews body of the speech

Content

_____ Speech is adapted to the audience's interests, knowledge, and attitudes

_____ Organization of speech is obvious and appropriate

_____ The main points are clearly identified

_____ Used appropriate transitions and internal summaries

_____ Evidence of research and support material (sources cited)

_____ Used acceptable logic, reasoning and emotional appeals

Delivery

_____ Establishes audience contact (eye contact, distance)

_____ Voice quality (not monotone, too soft, too fast, etc.)

_____ Used appropriate language and grammar

_____ Delivery is extemporaneous (conversational, did not read)

_____ Freedom from distractions (swaying, fidgeting, "um")

_____ Appropriate use of gestures, physical movement and visual aids

Conclusion

_____ Reminds audience of main points of speech

_____ Specifies precisely what the audience is to think or do in response to speech

_____ Ended strongly

Topic Selection and Time Requirement

_____ Topic is sufficiently narrowed and focused

_____ Observes time limit

Outline Evaluation Form

Attach the following checklist to your speech outline

Speaker _____   Topic _____

+ **excellent**   ✔ **competent**   - **needs improvement**

Title

_____ reflects the topic and generates interest

Specific Purpose

_____ is an infinitive phrase that expresses the intention of the speaker in terms of the audience

_____ is realistic and appropriate for the audience's interests, average knowledge level, and beliefs

Central Idea

_____ is a single, unambiguous sentence that expresses the central argument or idea that the speaker will develop

_____ makes a clear factual claim, is narrow, and is not vague

Introduction

_____ includes an attention getting statement

_____ establishes credibility

_____ links the topic to the audience

_____ previews the main ideas of the speech

Body

_____ follows the rules of formal outlining throughout, indenting correctly and using appropriate numbers and letters

_____ the main points provide logical and compelling support that further the central idea

_____ the subpoints represent well thought out examples, reasons, or arguments, accompanied by a cited source

Transitions

_____ located between the introduction and main body, between each main point of the speech, and between the body of the speech and its conclusion

Conclusion

_____ signals the end

_____ reaffirms your main points

_____ stresses the importance of your topic through a final statement (a clincher) that leaves a lasting impression in the minds of your listeners

Bibliography

_____ lists all sources cited in the body of the outline

_____ contains the required number of sources using APA format

Grammar

_____ complete sentences were used throughout the outline

_____ punctuation was accurate and all words were spelled correctly

Self-Analysis of Speech Evaluation

Name_____ Date _____

Speech Topic _____

Write a self-evaluation of the speech you have just given in class. Make sure your evaluation is objective and that it represents your true feelings about your performance. In the space provided make a list of strong and weak points you noticed in your speech.

Personal Evaluation of Speech

Strong Points   **Weak Points**

1.   1.

2.   2.

3.   3.

4.   4.

5.   5.

In a brief paragraph describe specific problems you encountered in your speech and suggest ways these problems might have been avoided or solved.

As a result of your instructor evaluation, peer evaluation, and self evaluation, list several positive steps you plan to take in your next speech to improve your communication evaluation.

SPEECHES #1, #2, #3

Peer Evaluations

_____
(Speaker's Name)

Suggested Grade: _____

Identify two speaker strengths on this factor:

_____

_____

_____

_____

Identify two areas in which the speaker could improve on this factor:

_____

_____

_____

_____

Other comments that might help the speaker do a better job:

_____

_____

_____

_____

_____
(Factor Evaluated)

_____
(Speaker's Name)

Suggested Grade: _____

Identify two speaker strengths on this factor:

_____

_____

_____

_____

Identify two areas in which the speaker could improve on this factor:

_____

_____

_____

_____

Other comments that might help the speaker do a better job:

_____

_____

_____

_____

_____
(Factor Evaluated)

_____
(Speaker's Name)

Suggested Grade: _____

Identify two speaker strengths on this factor:

_____

_____

_____

_____

Identify two areas in which the speaker could improve on this factor:

_____

_____

_____

_____

Other comments that might help the speaker do a better job:

_____

_____

_____

_____

_____
(Factor Evaluated)

(Speaker's Name)

Suggested Grade:

Identify two speaker strengths on this factor:

Identify two areas in which the speaker could improve on this factor:

Other comments that might help the speaker do a better job:

(Factor Evaluated)

(Speaker's Name)

Suggested Grade:

Identify two speaker strengths on this factor:

Identify two areas in which the speaker could improve on this factor:

Other comments that might help the speaker do a better job:

(Factor Evaluated)

(Speaker's Name)

Suggested Grade:

Identify two speaker strengths on this factor:

Identify two areas in which the speaker could improve on this factor:

Other comments that might help the speaker do a better job:

(Factor Evaluated)

_____
(Speaker's Name)

Suggested Grade: _____

Identify two speaker strengths on this factor:

_____
_____
_____
_____

Identify two areas in which the speaker could improve on this factor:

_____
_____
_____
_____

Other comments that might help the speaker do a better job:

_____
_____
_____
_____

_____
(Factor Evaluated)

_____
(Speaker's Name)

Suggested Grade: _____

Identify two speaker strengths on this factor:

_____
_____
_____
_____

Identify two areas in which the speaker could improve on this factor:

_____
_____
_____
_____

Other comments that might help the speaker do a better job:

_____
_____
_____
_____

_____
(Factor Evaluated)

_____
(Speaker's Name)

Suggested Grade: _____

Identify two speaker strengths on this factor:

_____
_____
_____
_____

Identify two areas in which the speaker could improve on this factor:

_____
_____
_____
_____

Other comments that might help the speaker do a better job:

_____
_____
_____
_____

_____
(Factor Evaluated)

Form 1

(Speaker's Name)

Suggested Grade:

Identify two speaker strengths on this factor:

_____

_____

Identify two areas in which the speaker could improve on this factor:

_____

_____

Other comments that might help the speaker do a better job:

_____

_____

(Factor Evaluated)

Form 2

(Speaker's Name)

Suggested Grade:

Identify two speaker strengths on this factor:

_____

_____

Identify two areas in which the speaker could improve on this factor:

_____

_____

Other comments that might help the speaker do a better job:

_____

_____

(Factor Evaluated)

Form 3

(Speaker's Name)

Suggested Grade:

Identify two speaker strengths on this factor:

_____

_____

Identify two areas in which the speaker could improve on this factor:

_____

_____

Other comments that might help the speaker do a better job:

_____

_____

(Factor Evaluated)

_____
(Speaker's Name)

Suggested Grade: _____

Identify two speaker strengths on this factor:

_____
_____
_____
_____

Identify two areas in which the speaker could improve on this factor:

_____
_____
_____
_____

Other comments that might help the speaker do a better job:

_____
_____
_____
_____

_____
(Factor Evaluated)

_____
(Speaker's Name)

Suggested Grade: _____

Identify two speaker strengths on this factor:

_____
_____
_____
_____

Identify two areas in which the speaker could improve on this factor:

_____
_____
_____
_____

Other comments that might help the speaker do a better job:

_____
_____
_____
_____

_____
(Factor Evaluated)

_____
(Speaker's Name)

Suggested Grade: _____

Identify two speaker strengths on this factor:

_____
_____
_____
_____

Identify two areas in which the speaker could improve on this factor:

_____
_____
_____
_____

Other comments that might help the speaker do a better job:

_____
_____
_____
_____

_____
(Factor Evaluated)

(Speaker's Name)

Suggested Grade: _____

Identify two speaker strengths on this factor:

_____

_____

_____

Identify two areas in which the speaker could improve on this factor:

_____

_____

_____

Other comments that might help the speaker do a better job:

_____

_____

_____

(Factor Evaluated)

(Speaker's Name)

Suggested Grade: _____

Identify two speaker strengths on this factor:

_____

_____

_____

Identify two areas in which the speaker could improve on this factor:

_____

_____

_____

Other comments that might help the speaker do a better job:

_____

_____

_____

(Factor Evaluated)

(Speaker's Name)

Suggested Grade: _____

Identify two speaker strengths on this factor:

_____

_____

_____

Identify two areas in which the speaker could improve on this factor:

_____

_____

_____

Other comments that might help the speaker do a better job:

_____

_____

_____

(Factor Evaluated)

(Speaker's Name)

Suggested Grade:

Identify two speaker strengths on this factor:

Identify two areas in which the speaker could improve on this factor:

Other comments that might help the speaker do a better job:

(Factor Evaluated)

(Speaker's Name)

Suggested Grade:

Identify two speaker strengths on this factor:

Identify two areas in which the speaker could improve on this factor:

Other comments that might help the speaker do a better job:

(Factor Evaluated)

(Speaker's Name)

Suggested Grade:

Identify two speaker strengths on this factor:

Identify two areas in which the speaker could improve on this factor:

Other comments that might help the speaker do a better job:

(Factor Evaluated)

(Speaker's Name)

Suggested Grade: _____

Identify two speaker strengths on this factor:

_____

_____

_____

Identify two areas in which the speaker could improve on this factor:

_____

_____

_____

Other comments that might help the speaker do a better job:

_____

_____

_____

_____
(Factor Evaluated)

(Speaker's Name)

Suggested Grade: _____

Identify two speaker strengths on this factor:

_____

_____

_____

Identify two areas in which the speaker could improve on this factor:

_____

_____

_____

Other comments that might help the speaker do a better job:

_____

_____

_____

_____
(Factor Evaluated)

(Speaker's Name)

Suggested Grade: _____

Identify two speaker strengths on this factor:

_____

_____

_____

Identify two areas in which the speaker could improve on this factor:

_____

_____

_____

Other comments that might help the speaker do a better job:

_____

_____

_____

_____
(Factor Evaluated)